D0486011

WOMAN ON DEATH ROW

VELMA BARFIELD

WOMAN ON DEATH ROW

P U B L I C A T I O N S
A ministry of the Billy Graham Association

1303 Hennepin Avenue
Minneapolis, Minnesota 55403

This edition is published with permission from the original publisher, Oliver-Nelson Books, P.O. Box 141000, Nashville, TN 37214.

Names of prisoners have been fictionalized for protection of privacy.

Scripture quotations are from the NEW KING JAMES VERSION. Copyright © 1979, 1980, 1982, Thomas Nelson Inc., Publishers.

Scripture quotations marked KJV are from the King James Version of the Bible.

Cover photograph and design by James T. Bricker.

Printed in the United States of America.

Library of Congress Cataloging in Publication Data

Barfield, Velma, 1932-1984.
  Woman on death row.

  1. Barfield, Velma, 1932-1984.   2. Female offenders—United States—
Biography.   3. Murder—United States—Case studies.   I. Title.
HV6248.B26A38   1985   364.1'523'0924 [B]   85-7289
ISBN 0-8407-9531-9 (pbk.)

CONTENTS

PREFACE

The Reverend Hugh Hoyle often talked to me about writing my story for publication. He gave me regular writing assignments which I completed, but he moved to Kansas before anything was worked out. I didn't think about a book again.

In one of her letters, Ruth Graham wrote that she believed my story needed to be told. She contacted Victor Oliver, president of Oliver-Nelson Books, and he came to visit me. After we talked, and I agreed to have the story published, he wrote, telling me that he was sending a professional writer, Cecil ("Cec") Murphey, to help me tell my story.

I want my story told because I hope it will help people understand what God can do in the life of one loathsome and desperate human being. I understand what the apostle meant when he called himself the chief of sinners. But, like Paul, I also have received the gift of God's love to change me.

I also want to make it clear that I am not blaming the drugs for my crimes. I am not blaming my troubled childhood or the marriage problems with Thomas. Someone said to me, "Velma, you had a lot of pain and hurt and anger and you never found any release for it. You kept pushing it back and it was like a time bomb. It finally went off and exploded." Maybe that's right. I don't know. I bear the responsibility for the wrongs I have done. I know those things influenced me, but they are my sins and my crimes.

During these past six and a half years in prison I have tried to help others find God in their lives. Because I know what He can do for me, I know what He can do for anyone. I also have been praying that my experiences with prescribed medication might also stand as a warning to other people before they become addicted as I did.

Velma Barfield
October 1984

FOREWORD

Finding God, or should I say, God finding her, was the powerful catalyst that turned Velma Barfield around.

In 1978, despairing of her crimes and drug addiction, she found God in prison. Until her 1984 execution, Velma powerfully influenced hundreds of people's lives.

After the initial confrontation with Jesus in her jail cell, she wrote to me,

"I wept and as I lay there weeping, I questioned could Jesus really love me, someone who had hurt so many people?

"And it was then it seemed He appeared with me in that cell answering my questions, saying, 'Yes, I do love you and I died on the cross for your sins, too. Won't you let me come and give you a brand new life?'

"Right then and there I asked Him into my life.... I confessed my sins to Him and I asked Him to forgive all my dirty past... He came into my life that night.... Ever since I've been telling others of His love—I can't hide it—I have to share it."

Ruth Bell Graham
January 1985

I have sinned exceedingly in
thought, word, and deed,
by my fault, by my own fault,
by my own most grievous fault.
Especially, I accuse myself of
the following sins…

from the Confession in the "Sacrament of Penance,"
St. Augustine's Prayer Book

WOMAN ON
DEATH ROW

1.

ACCUSATION

The doorbell rang persistently. Whoever was out there wouldn't go away. I made my way groggily across the room to the door. My head ached, and my knees were weak. I should have gotten up earlier, but I was just too tired. It was already mid-afternoon. When I opened the door I saw a man standing in front of me. I don't remember if he smiled. "Mrs. Barfield?"

I tried to focus on his face. "Yes?"

I didn't catch all the words, but I understood enough. "Detective Phillips. We'd like you to come to the police station for questioning."

"Questioning?" My stomach tightened. For a minute I didn't think I could breathe. Finally I said, "Questioning for what?"

"About the death of Stuart Taylor, ma'am."

"I—I don't know anything about—"

"Mrs. Barfield, if you'll just get dressed and come on down to the station, ma'am. We have some questions we need to ask you."

What am I going to say? Why are they questioning me? Are they going to charge me with Stuart's death? What's today? March 10, 1978. It has been weeks since Stuart's death, since late January. Why are they coming around now to question me? Has somebody accused me of doing something to him?

I felt scared and alone. I needed to talk to someone, but I

1

didn't know who. My mind wouldn't function. I couldn't figure out who to call.

I backed up and let the man inside. *I must look dragged out to him.* "I work nights at a nursing home and sleep during the day, and—"

"Yes, ma'am, we know," he said with a soft drawl, unlike the typical image of a detective. He sat down, obviously willing to wait for me.

Maybe I could ask him to leave and let me come later. No, he wouldn't agree to that. Even if he left, I'd still have to go down for questioning sometime. "I'll try not to take too long," I said as I headed for the bathroom.

I shut the door behind me and reached for my medication. Without bothering to use water to wash them down, I swallowed two Valium tranquilizers, two Tylenol with Codeine pain relievers, one Sinequan antidepressant, and one Elavil antidepressant. By habit, I leaned against the basin, waiting for the pills to take effect. *I can't leave with him until I get my wits about me. My medication will make me think more clearly. Or will I think less clearly after the pills go through my system? Will these pills only confuse me?* It took too much effort to reason that out. Only one thing was clear: under no circumstances could I function without help from my medication.

I don't know how long it took, but eventually I felt the calming effect. A kind of soft warmness came over me. My depression lifted momentarily. I had no idea how long they would keep me there. *What if it takes hours?* A sense of panic rose up inside me. *What will I do when it comes time for my next dosage?* I needed my medication with me. Hurriedly I thrust all my bottles of medication into my handbag. Just having it in my purse eased some of my anxiety, even though it occurred to me that I might be searched. I couldn't think of that now. Besides, I had gotten all my medications by legal prescription. We left the house and got into Mr. Phillips's car. New questions came pouring into my head, although now I was not nearly as terrified as when he had first come to the door. I tried to think of how I would answer. *I have to form clear and careful answers.* But my head felt fuzzy. I simply couldn't figure out anything to say.

Even so, it was one of my better days. Sometimes I went nearly a week without real clear-headedness. I managed to cope and had been coping all along, but most of the time I functioned without having to think about what I was doing.

Beyond my confusion and the dulling effect of medication, I was frightened. *What will they ask me? Do they have evidence I don't know about? Had they run some kind of special tests? Why have they come now?* Stuart had been dead since January 31. I wanted to ask why they had sent for me, especially now, but I was afraid to.

By the time we arrived at the Robeson county sheriff's department in Lumberton, the medication had dulled my high anxiety and fear. *This is nothing to get concerned about. Just some routine questioning.*

Inside the building, I saw a man I had gone to school with—Al Parnell. But I saw him only a second, so I wasn't absolutely sure. *He works for the sheriff's department, doesn't he? Or do I have him confused with somebody else? Wait a minute. I can't think about Al now.*

I followed Detective Phillips into a small room. He sat down and spread out several sheets of paper in front of him. He quietly filled out some kind of forms, all the while not saying anything.

His silence caused me to start getting anxious again. *I thought they wanted to question me. Why did they bring me here to sit like this? Some kind of test?* I wanted to scream or run from the room. *Maybe I could just get up and walk around. If I walk around, would that appear suspicious?* I couldn't decide, so I sat, waiting in agony.

"Mrs. Barfield, I'd like to read you your rights." He glanced at me and then quoted the statement as he must have done hundreds of times before. He stopped speaking and looked straight at me. Outside noises filtered into the room, sounding muffled and distorted. A phone kept ringing somewhere. *Why doesn't somebody answer that phone?* "Mrs. Barfield. You understand what's going on now, don't you?"

I nodded. He had read me my rights. "Yes."

"We have results of additional tests we did on the body of Stuart Taylor. The medical examiner reports the presence of arsenic."

Arsenic? Did I repeat the word? Or did the meaning bear down on me so heavily I thought I had?

"We believe the presence of arsenic in his body caused his death."

The shock must have shown on my face. I think my lips formed the words "arsenic" and "death" as if I could not relate the two. Yet I couldn't hear myself saying anything. A throbbing pain in my head blocked out his next few sentences. I needed to think. *I wish they'd leave me alone for awhile so I could straighten out my thoughts. What should I say now? What evidence does he have? Why does he want to question me about arsenic?* Nobody had said anything about additional tests being made. I'd never heard until now about arsenic showing up.

"Mrs. Barfield, you understand what I'm saying?" He paused. His blue eyes assured me that he found no pleasure in going through this.

I nodded.

"We have reason to believe that you killed Stuart Taylor."

"What kind of reasons?" I said, amazed at the calmness in my voice. *Or maybe I only masked my fear so well that the sound came out flat?* "Why would I want to do that?"

He turned momentarily toward his papers. Without looking up he said, "Death from arsenic poisoning, Mrs. Barfield. That's a serious charge. Poisoning means that you thought about it in advance, even planned it." I had felt frightened before, but now terror struck at me, gripping my throat and my stomach. *I've got to get out of this room. I've got to get away from him so that I can take another Valium. That will calm me down. It always calms me down. Maybe I can open my purse and try to slip a pill into my mouth without being noticed.*

"Mrs. Barfield? Do you understand what I'm saying? We have reason to believe that you—"

"What kind of reasons?" I asked and then stopped. *Hadn't he said those words before? Is he trying to trick me?* I closed my mouth, determined not to say anything.

For nearly three hours, Mr. Phillips kept probing, asking questions, coming back to the first things he asked. *Why is he doing this? Is he trying to trick me into saying something stupid?* I denied everything. One time I blurted out, "Stuart and I were engaged to be married."

"But you had a quarrel?"

"Lots of people quarrel, but they don't kill each other," I said, proud of my quick response.

How long did he question me? I think almost three hours, but it seemed more like eight. He finally stood up and said, "Guess that's all, Mrs. Barfield. For now."

He's letting me go. They have no evidence against me or they wouldn't let me leave like this.

On the drive home, nobody said anything. I didn't want to talk anyway. Despite his letting me go, I felt terrible inside, and it didn't have anything to do with the medication. I couldn't recall ever feeling good inside.

I didn't think it all out then. But looking back, guilt pressed heavily on me all the time, like a wire around the top of my head that kept getting tighter and tighter. Taking medication was the only thing that relieved some of that guilt. I had felt guilty about something all my life. And dirty. Like I wasn't fit to be around other people. Most of all, I despised myself— and had for a long time. Maybe all of my life. No matter what I did or didn't do, I always felt guilty about everything.

Mr. Phillips let me off at the house. I sighed in relief when he drove away. They hadn't arrested me, and they hadn't charged me. *Maybe that questioning was the last of it.* I tried to convince myself, but inside I knew different.

I went to work that night, from 11:00 until 7:00 the next morning, my usual shift at the nursing home. I didn't tell anyone there about the questioning.

I worked listlessly, but I functioned. I had been functioning on the job for months. I had brought my medication with me, something I usually didn't do. The police had not searched me, and I still had all of my medication. Now I faced an eight-hour shift with frayed nerves and a deep-seated restlessness. I wanted my medication near me. I don't think anyone at the nursing home knew I was on medication. At least no one ever said anything.

That night I took four Valium tranquilizers—twice my normal dose. But I told myself that this time I had good reason for the extra. I still felt a deep sense of grief over Stuart's death. So many strange emotions struggled inside me. Guilt. Grief. Anxiety. Loneliness. All kinds of emotions were mixed up together. My medication was the only way I could find relief from them.

Saturday morning after getting off work, I drove to my son Ronnie's house instead of going home. At the time he lived in Lumberton too. Ronnie is the older of my two children, and he always seemed to understand me. I had always been able to talk a lot of things out with him.

"Ronnie, a funny thing happened yesterday." I told him about going to the sheriff's department and about all the questions. "I don't know why they want me to say I'm guilty." I looked at him, well over six feet tall, thin, dark complexioned with pitch-black hair, just like his daddy, Thomas Burke. "What will I do if they want to charge me with Stuart's death?"

"It'll work out all right, Mama," he said.

"You know Stuart and I had our problems all along, but they're saying somebody gave him arsenic and that he died from that."

"Where would you get hold of something like arsenic?" His words comforted me. Just to have him listen helped me forget about the ordeal of the day before. But I knew I had to think ahead. If they came back to question me again, I wanted to be ready.

As soon as I got home I called an attorney that I knew of in Fayetteville. Even though it was Saturday, I was able to locate him. I explained what had happened and then asked, "If they charge me, would you represent me?"

"Why don't you call me back if they do charge you?"

Not sure what that meant, I refused to dwell on it, assuming he was giving me a partial acceptance if they charged me. *If they charge me. If they had evidence, they could have charged me on Friday. Maybe they have nothing. What could they have against me?*

I tried to comfort myself by thinking that they hadn't actually charged me with anything. *If they thought I had done it, wouldn't they have arrested me right then? Or wouldn't they have warned me or something?* No matter how hard I tried to reason it out, though, I couldn't feel any peace.

I took some Dalmane sleeping pills on top of my regular medication, but I still hardly slept that entire weekend. I worked both Saturday and Sunday nights, and when I went to bed on Monday morning, I rested badly. My mind was filled with all kinds of fears and thoughts. *What will happen next? What if they actually charge me? What if I go on trial? What if—* I drifted off to sleep, but I awakened a short time later with the same thoughts. I lay on the bed fully awake and very depressed. My anxieties and fears were tormenting me so badly that I thought of doing away with myself. I considered taking enough medication to sink into a peaceful nothingness with no pain—ever again. No more tormenting thoughts, no more problems, no more self-hatred. *It would be so easy. It would solve everything.*

I dumped the contents from all my medicine bottles into a Kleenex tissue that I held in my hand. The best I remember, I planned to gulp them all down. I must have fallen asleep instead. I knew nothing until a pounding on the door woke me. I still clutched the tissue filled with my pills. Rousing myself out of a drugged sleep, I opened my eyes and saw Ronnie standing over me. He was looking at the doubled up tissue and pills in my hand.

"Give them to me, Mama." Without waiting for me to respond, he reached over and took them. He counted them. Twenty-one. He looked at me. "Did you have any thoughts of taking all of them?"

I didn't want to look at him. I didn't want him to see my pitiful state. "I don't know. I think I planned to flush them down the toilet," I lied, "and fell asleep with them in my hand."

"Mama," he said, putting the pills in his pocket, "I want you to listen now. They're coming after you. Today sometime."

"Who's coming?" But, of course, I knew the answer.

"The police."

The clock showed 3:35. *How could I have slept so long and yet be so tired?*

"Mama, people have been talking all weekend. They think you're responsible for Stuart's death. I know the police are going to arrest you today. It would be better for you if you went down there on your own."

"Arrest me?" I said. A terrible fear gripped me. I wanted to go back to bed, to get under the covers, to go to sleep and forget everything. But Ronnie's words had gotten through to me. The police had decided I was responsible for Stuart's death. I began to cry.

Ronnie was already crying as he talked to me and tried to calm me down. He took my hand. "Come on, Mama, let me take you down there."

If my mind had really been clear I would have asked how he knew the police planned to arrest me. I would have asked who had been talking all weekend. But my head ached and my stomach felt like one large knot tightening itself.

Ronnie refused to let me out of his sight as I stumbled through the bedroom, getting dressed to let him take me to the police station.

I didn't argue with Ronnie; I just did what he said. I followed him out to the car and let him drive me to the same building where Detective Phillips had questioned me. I didn't see Mr. Phillips this time, but a detective named Lovett took me to the same tiny room in which I had been questioned on Friday. I was surprised at how kind he seemed—and how patient.

He informed me of my rights and then said, "I know this is unpleasant, but we have good reason to believe that you poisoned Stuart Taylor sometime around the end of January." He talked a little longer and finally he said quietly, "Mrs. Bar-field, did you poison Stuart Taylor?" I couldn't look him in the face, but I answered his question.

"Yes."

2.

CONFESSION

"You poisoned Stuart Taylor, didn't you?"

Mr. Lovett kept on asking the same questions. I tried to answer as clearly as I could. From the time Ronnie brought me to the police station, I knew that denying the charges or lying wouldn't do any good. They knew—somehow they knew—so I decided not to deny anything.

"Yes."

"You deliberately killed Stuart Taylor with arsenic."

"I didn't—didn't mean to kill him—I just wanted to make him sick. I needed time to—"

"But you did use arsenic?"

"Yes."

"Where did you get the arsenic?"

"I didn't use arsenic."

"What did you use then?"

"Just poison."

"There have been others, too?" he asked.

I've never been sure why he asked that question. Did he know something else? Was he guessing? Was it only a routine kind of thing that detectives asked in their interrogation? I didn't know, and in fact I didn't even think of it at the time. I was confused. I wished that I had called that Fayetteville attorney before coming in with Ronnie.

"There have been others?" he repeated.

"Yes."

"Want to tell me about it?"

I talked for a long time after that, telling him everything as clearly as my fuzzy mind would let me. I tried not to hold anything back. It didn't matter any more. They knew enough or they wouldn't have planned to arrest me. Why shouldn't I tell them everything?

Later another man came in. I looked up and saw Al Parnell and felt a sense of relief. "Hello, Al," I managed to say.

Al nodded, smiled, and said, "Hello, Velma." It must have made him uncomfortable to question me. Al had been a grade behind me in school in Parkton, and we had known each other most of our lives. In small North Carolina towns like Lumberton and Parkton, all the people know each other.

After greeting me, he didn't seem to know if he ought to shake my hand or not. He just sat down. "Velma, I need to ask you a few questions."

I nodded, letting him know I would answer anything. His questions sounded almost the same as the detective before him.

"Tell me about the poison. Where did you buy the arsenic?"

"It wasn't arsenic," I corrected him. "I bought it at—" I stopped, my mind confused. "Or was it— No, no, let me think. I had just gone to the doctor for my checkup—or was that another time?" My mind wouldn't function properly, and it seemed important that I tell the truth.

Al never spoke harshly or showed any signs of impatience with my stumbling answers. He waited when my mind went blank, and he sympathized when I broke down and cried.

Later Al himself took me through the fingerprinting and the booking procedure. He must have volunteered to do all this because when he got ready to drive me over to the county jail, Detective Lovett asked, "Want me to do that for you?"

He shook his head. "No, I'll take her there by myself." He turned to me and said, "My car's parked right outside."

We went out of the building to get into the car. Al opened the door for me as if we had been out together. He didn't handcuff me either. Al talked as friendly as always while he drove the one block to the Robeson county jail. He even asked about one of my brothers.

The women's section of the jail was located on the second floor. Al walked alongside the officer who took me to the women's cell block. While the officer was getting me settled in, Al said, "I'll be back in a little while."

I don't remember if I asked him anything but he said, "I've been on the phone with both of your kids. Kim seems especially concerned, and Ronnie told me about your medication. Of course, they're worried about you. Anyway, I told them I'd do what I could for you. We've called your doctor. I'm going out now to the drugstore to get your prescription filled."

When Al returned, he handed me the two tablets prescribed by the doctor. I didn't even ask what they were. I needed that medication. If he hadn't handed me a Coke to wash them down, I would have swallowed them dry. Over the years of taking medication, I had learned to do that with ease.

Al also brought me a hamburger and fries. That simple act of thoughtfulness touched me.

"Thanks, Al, but I can't eat anything. I'm not hungry. Honest—"

"Try to eat something."

It had been at least eighteen hours since I had eaten, but I had no desire for food. "I—I can't."

"Just try," he said. He pulled up a chair and sat down outside my cell and waited for me to eat. I felt nauseated. I didn't want food and wondered if I would ever want to eat anything again.

"I promised your kids that I would take care of you. Velma, I want you to eat this food. You'll feel better if you do."

"I can't. Not now."

"Just try."

To please Al—and to avoid having him contact Ronnie or my daughter Kim—I decided to try to eat. I didn't want the kids to worry about anything, especially my not getting enough to eat.

After he saw me take a few bites, he was satisfied. Al got

up. "I'll come by and see you a little while in the morning." Then he left.

I swallowed what I had eaten and had to steel myself against vomiting it back up. I didn't want food. I just wanted to be left alone in my private misery. Before Al left, the medication he brought me had begun to take effect. I could feel myself relaxing.

I had hardly slept since Friday. The effect of that medication, plus all that I had taken earlier, seemed to work on me at once. I stumbled over to the hard bunk and lay down. I must have fallen asleep immediately. That night, alone in the jail cell, I slept soundly. I didn't know a thing until 7:00 the next morning when the head jailer woke me.

"Some of your family's downstairs," he said. He handed me a glass of water and more of the medication Al had brought the night before. "Better get cleaned up and I'll take you down."

Minutes later I walked downstairs and saw my sister Arlene and her husband who had come from Charleston, South Carolina. Kim and her husband, Dennis Norton, had also come.

As soon as I saw them, I broke into tears. They started to cry too. All at once, we started talking at the same time to each other. Then someone broke down, and we all started crying again. As painful as it was to face my family after being charged with the murder, it also comforted me. Knowing the charge against me, they still had come.

The jailer let me stay for about an hour with them. During that time, they never asked me about Stuart's death, my arrest, or anything that had happened. But they did the most wonderful thing in the world—they supported me and let me know they cared.

"We've been talking to the jailer," Arlene said just before I had to leave. "He told us you'd be going to court today. They have to appoint you an attorney. When we leave here, we're going over to Kim and Dennis's, and then we'll see you back in court."

The jailer took me back to the cell when my family left. Despite all the sleep I'd had, I still felt groggy and confused. I tried to remember everything about the day before, but pieces seemed to be missing. I knew about Ronnie taking me to the police and my ending up in jail, but most of the details had disappeared. That didn't distress me too much because I had lived that way for a long time. I often had memory lapses. Some days passed without the slightest awareness of what I had done during the entire time.

The medication I had received that morning drained all my energy. As soon as I got back into the cell, I stumbled over to my bunk and immediately fell asleep again.

About 8:45, the same morning, the bailiff came to take me to the courthouse. Just before we left, the guard brought me additional medication that had been prescribed. I stammered a word of thanks to him. I knew that I was going to need every bit of help I could get. But the impact of the situation had not hit me yet, even though I had cried with the family. I had brought shame upon them. I always seemed to cause my family shame. But I had felt guilty for so long for so many things that my arrest didn't make much difference to my thinking.

The bailiff escorted me to the courthouse. He put me in a little room with some other people who also were waiting to appear before the judge. A little later, Al opened the door and looked around until he saw me. He motioned with his hand and called my name. "Velma." I had been sitting by myself in a corner of the room. I may even have gone back to sleep because I had the hardest time staying awake. I don't remember anything from the time the bailiff left me there until Al came to the door. Wearily, I got up and walked to where he stood. It took all my energy just to move across the room. I wondered if I had ever felt so tired in my entire life. It never occurred to me that the medication caused my sluggishness. In those days, I rarely made a connection between the medications and my responses.

"Velma, I've talked to the judge. I asked him if, while you're waiting, you could be alone with your family in one of these rooms, and he agreed."

That simple gesture touched me because Al didn't have to go out of his way to do that for me. I felt grateful and, at the same time, too tired to care much about anything that happened.

A guard led us into a room no one else was using, where I could be alone with the family. Those few minutes with my family made me feel better and not quite so alone. I saw my brothers Jesse and John, my sister Arlene, and my two children, Ronnie and Kim. There may have been others, but my mind was so fuzzy that it was hard just trying to keep their faces in focus. The medication given me before leaving the jail worked so well that everything kept going in and out of focus as we talked.

Even though I wanted them with me, at the same time, I desperately wanted them to leave me alone so I could go to sleep. I was as exhausted as if I had worked twenty-four straight hours. I couldn't understand my tiredness. I had slept soundly the night before. As I look back, I can understand why so few emotions surfaced over the proceedings. Between the medication and my state of shock, it was almost as if I were watching something happening to someone else.

At noon they returned me to the jail because the judge had not gotten around to my case. A guard gave me more medication before I lay down on the hard bunk. I fell asleep almost immediately. I didn't know a thing until the bailiff woke me to go back to court.

At the courthouse that afternoon, I was put in a room by myself. I was so groggy that no matter how hard I tried, I couldn't pull myself fully awake. I may have fallen asleep while waiting for them to call me.

When I finally went into the courtroom, the judge told me that the court had appointed an attorney for me. The attorney introduced himself as Bob Jacobson. I hardly saw him then, I was so dazed.

Bob Jacobson took me to a holding room to talk for a few minutes. I listened and tried to concentrate, but only about half his words got through to me. I did understand that the judge had said they were sending me to the Dorothea Dix State Hospital in Raleigh for a psychiatric evaluation to determine whether I was mentally competent to stand trial.

He must have sensed that I didn't follow most of what he tried to explain. He finally said, "I want to talk to your family before they get away." As he left, he told the guard to put me in the holding room again.

While waiting in the holding room for him to come back or for the guard to take me to the jail, I lay down on a couch and drifted off to sleep. That must have been about 4:30.

It was 6:00 when the guard woke me. "Mrs. Barfield, I'm taking you back to the jail now."

"I'm supposed to wait here for my lawyer," I said, certain that Mr. Jacobson had said he would come back and talk to me again. "He just went out to talk to my family and he'll be back in a minute—"

"I'm sorry, ma'am, but your lawyer has gone and so has everybody else. I'm supposed to take you back to the jail."

"You're sure?" I was convinced that Bob Jacobson had planned to talk to me some more. I had no idea about what. But it seemed like too much effort to argue since the tiredness had not left me. I got up to go with him.

As we walked out of the building, I kept trying to remember if Mr. Jacobson had said he would return or not. I thought he had said he would, but then maybe I had misunderstood that along with a lot of other things. "You're sure?" I asked the guard again.

I should have been able to answer my own question. The building was almost vacant except for two or three stragglers, and it was dark outside. But I didn't reason very well. I'm not sure that the guard even answered me that time.

Almost as soon as I got back inside my cell, I was handed another dose of medication. Within minutes, I left everything behind as I slipped drowsily into my own quiet dream world.

I never had to go without medication from the time I first went to the county jail in Lumberton, even through my time at Dorothea Dix State Hospital. When I got to Dix on

Wednesday, March 15, 1978, I slept through the afternoon and didn't wake up until the next morning. I only got up when someone roused me for meals and medication. I settled into a routine of sleep, followed by meals and medication, followed by sleep, followed by meals and medication again. I slept constantly, or so it seemed. I had only a vague awareness of night and morning and then night again.

I don't remember very much of what happened those first few days, except for meeting a nice doctor.

When he introduced himself, I liked the warm smile he gave me. He didn't seem like a doctor to me, although I don't know why.

He shook my hand and we had a friendly chat about how I felt. He asked me, "How have they been treating you here at Dorothea Dix?"

"All right," I answered because they had not mistreated me and I didn't have anything to complain about.

He stayed and talked to me awhile. He asked me questions such as, "You understand that you poisoned Stuart Taylor?" "You knew what you were doing?" "You know why the court sent you here?"

I didn't want to evade answering him, but I was so groggy that I couldn't force my thoughts together. I don't know if all my answers made sense.

I was kept at the state hospital for almost five weeks. The assigned doctor talked with me occasionally, asking such questions as, "Why do you need such large amounts of medication?"

I had no way to explain *why*. I think I finally said, "Because I need the medications. They help me to keep going."

Even though I was medicated three times a day at the hospital, I was given less than I had been taking. All during my entire stay at Dix I suffered from withdrawal. Some days, of course, were worse than others. I'd feel myself drawing up on the inside, and I'd get all sweaty and nervous. I couldn't stand to be sitting close to people, and I wanted to be by myself as much as possible. I felt faint and kept wondering if I would pass out. My skin itched inside, and I couldn't do anything about it. I'd beg, "Please, give me something to calm my nerves. Just anything. My nerves are driving me crazy."

One Friday afternoon, maybe after I had been at Dix for three weeks, I had the worst time of all. My hands acted as if they were drawing backwards, drawing up into a tight ball. The nerves inside my arms throbbed and pulled at me, as if fighting against my skin as it tried to tighten up. I tried to lie down, or to sit, and even to walk around, but nothing helped. My arms tingled, and I didn't think I could stand much more of it. I finally collapsed on my bed, thinking I could go to sleep. But sleep refused to come.

"I don't feel good," I told the lady who stayed in the same room with me.

"What's wrong?"

I tried to explain how I felt and wondered if I even made sense. "I just don't feel good, and now I'm getting real fainty."

"Take a shower. You'll feel better," she said.

I didn't want a shower. My system wanted additional medication and I knew it. But I was so desperate, I would try anything.

She helped me into the shower right across the hall. Even though I took a cold shower and then a hot one, I still felt bad, maybe a little worse because now I had a lot of pain in my head.

When the supper call came, I told the other lady, "I'm not going down to eat supper because everytime I move, I feel like I'm going to faint."

She went on to the dining room, and I lay on the bed. The pain in my head increased. It felt as if someone were hammering at my skull. At the same time, the drawing in my arms brought tears to my eyes because it hurt so bad. The symptoms got worse and began to affect my breathing. Every time I inhaled, a stab of pain went through my chest, my head, and my arms. That scared me, and before long I was afraid I wouldn't get my next breath.

Either I called for the head nurse or my roommate did. I

can't remember, except that the head nurse did come down to the room. "What's wrong?"

I tried to explain to her how bad I felt. She looked at me and made me get dressed again. She took me by the arm so that I could walk straight, and we went down to the examining room.

The doctor on duty examined me and asked a few questions. I told him how bad I felt.

"I want you to stay in bed until morning," he said when I finished.

"But I need something for the pain. Please, give me something, anything. I can't keep taking this."

"You go on back to your room and get into bed. Stay there and you'll feel better by morning."

"Just anything. A shot of Demerol. A Valium or—"

"Just go on back to your room. I don't want you out in the dayroom," he said. "Go to bed now."

Although it was only a little past 7:00 P.M., I did what he said. I stayed in my room all night, but I was restless and didn't sleep much. The symptoms didn't get any better.

By the time the call came to go down to breakfast on Saturday morning, I felt worse. All the symptoms struck—the dizziness, the sweatiness, and the faintness. My head throbbed so bad I didn't want to keep my eyes open.

I didn't go down to the dining room. I had no appetite, and I was sure that I would pass out if I tried to walk that far. Instead I walked into the dayroom and sat down. The dizziness and the sweatiness increased.

A technician who was walking down the hall saw me. "How are you feeling today, Mrs. Barfield?"

"I feel funny. Like something's very wrong." I tried to explain to him how I felt.

"Come on down to the office," he said as he helped me out of the chair. "Let me check your blood pressure."

After he checked it, he said, "I don't think you ought to go into the dining room this morning. I'll have someone bring breakfast to your room."

I didn't want to eat anything, but they brought me a tray anyway. I managed to get down a few swallows of coffee. When my roommate came back after breakfast, I felt worse than I had the day before. "Please—call a nurse," I begged.

Minutes later a nurse came into the room and looked me over. She sent for the doctor and yelled to another nurse, "Bring the blood pressure pump!"

By then, I could hear them speaking in nervous, high-pitched voices, but I couldn't answer. It took all my effort to draw each breath. My head felt as if it would explode from the pain. Perspiration was pouring off me.

The doctor on call came rushing down the hall. Someone strapped the blood pressure pump on my arm and left it there. The doctor's voice, in an effort to sound calm, said, "I'm going to give you a shot."

He stuck a needle into my left arm but couldn't find a vein. He tried the other arm. My breathing was getting even more shallow. I wanted to scream, "Hurry! I can't keep breathing!" My whole left side felt as if it were drawing up on me.

The doctor finally found a vein, and I could feel something going into my arm. I don't know what it was. I think it was Benadryl. In a short while the drawing feeling quit, and I stopped perspiring. I didn't have to concentrate on consciously breathing, and I could even talk a little.

"Thanks," I managed to say. "I'm better now."

"You know, lady, anytime you feel like this, don't you hesitate to let somebody know."

"I did tell somebody. I told the nurse last night."

"Anyway, your blood pressure got dangerously high. You don't want that to happen again," he said. I don't know whether he had heard me.

I didn't have any more trouble with my blood pressure, but after that, they also kept me well medicated. Yet even with the increased medication, the whole time at Dix I felt nervous, edgy, and restless. I didn't sleep well. Several times I had spells of heavy perspiring.

My lawyer came to see me at least once. He started talking, and then stopped. "Don't you know who I am?"

I hadn't remembered him. He tried to make everything clear to me and to explain what was happening. I listened, but I don't think most of it sank in.

He came on Wednesday, and I was released on the following Monday to go back to jail.

When I left the state hospital, I stared at the trees as we drove away. I had been inside about five weeks. During that period of time, I had not paid attention to anything outside of myself. The leaves had filled out the stark barrenness of the winter trees, and I saw green everywhere. So beautiful. *But I can't touch the leaves or get close to the flowers.* I realized it was the middle of April, a lovely time of year in North Carolina.

Facts were beginning to filter through to me. It would soon be May. The judge had set the trial to begin the last week of November. *That's more than half a year away. What will I do with myself during that time? They will never let me go home to wait—not on a charge of murder.*

After I was returned to the jail, I had to appear in court a number of times. The judge refused to set bond. At one appearance, we asked for a change of venue, but he refused. We went back again, and then they moved the trial from Lumberton to Laurinburg. Later they moved it to Elizabethtown, North Carolina.

Al Parnell and Mr. Lovett brought me back to the Lumberton jail. I was confined alone in a cell designed for four people. I heard voices and saw people only as they passed by. I stayed alone through each long day until November.

I had nothing to read, although occasionally somebody would give me a newspaper. Kim and Ronnie visited me regularly. I had a Bible at home and asked Ronnie if he would bring it to me. The Bible was one of the few books we were allowed to keep in jail.

Depression hit me during the first few days back in jail. I was still taking medication. The city must have paid for it. It was a smaller amount than I had been taking on my own and even smaller than the decreased daily amounts I had received at Dorothea Dix. After a few days I experienced some withdrawal symptoms.

Worse than the chemical withdrawal, however, was my increased awareness of every wrong thing I had ever done. I found myself reliving my whole life. The more I dwelt on it, the more I hated myself. I began to relive the wrong things I had done and think about everything that had happened. Because I was still taking medication, I still wasn't thinking things out clearly. But I knew what I had done, and I didn't like one thing about myself. *I'm the most contemptible person in the world. The world would be better off without me.* At times I thought about how easy it would be if I took my life. And if I had figured out the way to do it, I would have. I was miserable. It seemed to me that everyone knew everything about me, as if I wore some kind of sign that told people everything.

I didn't want to see anyone, not even my brothers and sisters who traveled a long way to get there. I didn't care about them and convinced myself that nobody cared about me. Not a single person in the whole world really was concerned. Why should anyone care?

Ronnie and Kim both lived in Lumberton, and they came to see me regularly. I suppose when I kept thinking about nobody caring, I didn't think about them. Other than family members, I refused to talk to anyone. Even when relatives came to visit, I felt wretched the whole time.

Despite my refusal to see them, people still tried to get in. "You don't care about me!" I screamed in imaginary conversation to such people. "You only want information. You want all the details, but you don't care!"

I was bitter, and I was angry. Mostly I was angry with myself. *Velma, you're the most miserable person in the world. How could you let these things happen? You don't deserve to live, and nobody cares. You don't deserve to have anyone care for you.* That's how I talked to myself most of the time.

The longer I stayed in that cell, the more realistic my situation became. I didn't think much about the trial because that didn't matter. Or at least I didn't care what happened. I hated myself, my whole life, and the rest of the world.

I screamed. "They're out to get me. They'll do everything and anything to get me!" I probably didn't make sense half the time. I had so messed up my thinking that I couldn't feel anything except hatred, anger, and bitterness.

Suicide continued to cross my mind regularly. As I look back, I still have no idea why I didn't try to kill myself. I only knew one thing: I didn't want to live.

3.

DARK SIDE OF INNOCENCE

Why do people talk about childhood as the happy time in life? We have all these ideas about the innocence of youth and their carefree life. Maybe that's true for some. It wasn't true for me.

I was born in Cumberland county, North Carolina, on Saturday, October 29, 1932. I was named Margie Velma Bullard, but nobody ever called me anything but Velma. I was the second child with only my brother Olive older.

We had nine children in the family, with the twins Ray and Fay (the last ones) born when I was fourteen. I don't remember much about my early childhood. We lived in the country at first, outside Wade, North Carolina. In those days Daddy had a small farm which his daddy left him when he died. Only a few acres, but it was Daddy's. Later he sold it when we moved into another county, but still in the country.

I was afraid of my daddy, Murphy Bullard, even while still a small child. He had a violent temper, and none of us wanted to be around when he blew up. He was only about five feet seven, but he was heavyset.

I used to wonder why my mother put up with him and his hot temper. When Daddy couldn't find a hammer in the place where he thought it ought to be, he would explode. He'd throw chairs across the room or pull drawers out of chests and scatter the contents everywhere. His anger erupted when anything at home crossed him.

The smallest things triggered his violence. He usually took

24

out his anger on us kids as well as the furniture. More than once, a rage came over him, and he threw all the food off the table. Another time I saw him grab a beautiful bedspread that Mama especially liked. He stood in the middle of the bedroom and ripped it to shreds.

I don't remember that Daddy drank a lot—and often he didn't touch a drop for weeks at a time—but when he drank he got even meaner and more high-tempered.

Mama was the most patient woman in the world. She stood as tall as Daddy but was slim. As I got older, I used to ask, "Mama, why do you put up with him? Why do you stay with him like this?"

One time, when I was maybe twelve, she said, "I don't have nowhere to go if I did leave him."

"I'd sure find someplace else to go! And I will, too, when I get older!"

That ended the conversation, but it angered me that she put up with it. Her willingness to stay with Daddy was something I just couldn't understand.

Shortly before she died, Mama often said wistfully, "I wish I could take back some years."

The first few times she said those words, I didn't know exactly what she meant. From the way she said it, though, I wondered if she meant that she wished she had never married Daddy in the first place. But back in those days, marriage was about the only choice a woman had. Even after we were grown, Mama had no skills and couldn't have found work easily.

Daddy treated Olive worse than he treated me. Olive got beatings with anything Daddy could lay his hands on. Sometimes Daddy used his belt or a big stick. The worst beating Olive ever got scared me. Daddy picked up the back bend that goes across a mule, and he started hitting away at Olive until the blood ran. I screamed and felt so sorry for Olive. Although Daddy never beat me like that, from then on, I was afraid of him. Whenever he beat me, I'd see in my mind how bad Olive looked that time and I feared he'd do the same to me.

We moved around some, but always we lived in the same

area. And, with a family of eleven, none of us had much privacy no matter where we lived. Most of the time, through high school, I slept in the same bedroom with my parents.

A lot of nights I woke up hearing my mother scream. Daddy didn't hit her, but he would grab her arm and twist it until she screamed from the pain. Sometimes he grabbed a finger and did the same thing. Mama never fought back.

Most of the time while I was growing up, Daddy worked the second shift at a textile mill where he fixed looms. He left for the plant before I got home from school, and he didn't get back until close to midnight. During the week I didn't have to see a lot of him.

I grew up both hating and fearing him as much as I loved him. I guess it's horrible to say that, but most of the time he was mean and cruel. At times I felt the same way toward Mama because she let him get away with it, and I always thought mothers should defend their children. In a way, I seemed to accept Daddy's high-tempered ways because I thought that's the way men are. But Mama never acted like I thought mamas ought to. Mamas should love their children and stand up for them, and Mama never stood up for me, or for any of us, at least not while I still lived with them.

Later in life I realized that she did try to intervene now and then, but it never did any good. If anything, it only made Daddy act worse. He'd brush her aside and say, "Lillie, you just stay out of this. I gotta teach that kid a lesson!"

When I walked home from school in the afternoons, I liked to pretend that not only was Daddy at work, but that he wouldn't ever come home again. During school hours, I forgot him and the house and all the hard work I had to do. But just as soon as I started down the street to go home, it all came back to me again. Pretending wasn't enough. I knew that Daddy would be home again at midnight.

Those kind of feelings, even by the time I was ten, had built up inside me. It might have been better if I could have talked to someone about how things were at home, but I didn't have anyone. Even though I had cousins who lived nearby, I couldn't talk to them about how I felt.

In the section of North Carolina where I grew up, people didn't go talking to other people about their problems. What went on inside the home stayed inside. I did the only thing I knew how to do—I kept it all inside me. Over the years, the feelings got worse and worse.

Besides not having anyone to talk to, I didn't think anyone would believe me. The community looked up to my daddy. He treated the neighbors fine and did anything he could to help any of them. It would have been hard for them to believe the things he did because he only did them at home with just the family around. I guess his sister saw it a few times, but she was part of the family.

Daddy wasn't always bad-tempered, however. I remember when I was about ten or eleven that sometimes, when he was sitting in his favorite chair and I would be walking by, he would grab me and pull me up on his lap and hold me. I loved that closeness and warmth. I never told anyone how much it meant to me.

We moved to Robeson county, on the Parkton route, when I was thirteen. A few months later, I stayed home from school because I didn't feel well. A lot of flu was going around, and so I decided to stay in bed all day.

Mama was outside working in the yard. Daddy walked into the room and saw me lying there. Without saying a word, he came over to the bed and raped me. I was scared, but I tried to fight back my fears. I didn't want to say or do anything that would get him mad.

When he was finished, he just got up and left the room. He never did say anything. I wanted to tell somebody, but I didn't know who. I thought about telling Mama, but I didn't think she would believe me. Or if she believed me, I was afraid she'd think I had wanted him to do it.

I was confused and didn't know what to do. I lay in bed a long time and cried—quietly—because I didn't want anyone to hear me and ask what was wrong.

When I went to supper that evening I couldn't even look at Daddy. All I thought about was how dirty and awful I was.

As much as I hated Daddy, I also loved him. My feelings were so mixed up, and I was ashamed of how I felt. I couldn't tell my brothers and sisters—how could I admit that I deeply loved a father who did the kind of things he did to me?

One time Mama made out a grocery list and told Daddy, "You'll have to do the shopping today. Take Velma along with you."

I was so excited to go with Daddy to the store, although I carefully hid my joy.

Daddy gave me the list and monies for groceries and he went somewhere else. I bought everything just as Mama had written down. After putting the groceries in the car, and while I waited for Daddy, I went into a department store to browse.

I saw what had to have been the most beautiful dress ever: a vivid pink floral cotton. The dress was plain except for a three-inch ruffle across the hem. I walked around that mannequin, finally touching the soft ruffle, wishing I owned a dress like that.

At the same time, I knew I could never have that dress. I seldom had new clothes, and when I got anything new, Mama always bought it. But I couldn't stop thinking about that beautiful dress.

When I met Daddy, I blurted out, "Oh, Daddy, I saw the most wonderful pink dress! Come on, let me show you!" I grabbed his arm and half pulled him to the store.

He looked at the dress and then at me. "Real nice, Velma."

"And the ruffle. Why, it must be at least three inches wide!" After examining it carefully once again, I started to walk away, to go back home.

"Velma, you really like it?"

"Oh, Daddy, I think it's the most beautiful thing!"

"You go back inside and buy it. I'll give you the money." He counted out the dollars and put them in my hand.

After buying the dress I still had change left and he said, "Keep it. You can use it." Daddy had never done that before— or again—that I remembered.

I wonder if Daddy ever knew the pleasure he gave me that

day. Of all the days of my childhood, that is the happiest day I can remember.

All the way home, I talked about the dress. I could hardly wait to get home to show my friends and my cousins. When I showed Mama, she didn't say much, except something like, "That ruffle will make a lot of extra work pressing it all the time."

I walked away from her. I wasn't going to let her spoil my joy over that dress. And no matter how many clothes I bought afterward, in my thinking, nothing ever looked so beautiful as that pink dress with the floral pattern.

As my affection grew for Daddy, I seemed to dislike Mama more, although I couldn't put any of those things into words. Only during the years in prison, isolated from others and alone much of the time, have I taken my life apart and seen things I never understood before. Over and over I've asked, Where did it all start? I keep coming up with the same answer: It started back as far as I can remember. That's why I'm going into many childhood memories.

Occasionally Olive and I got into scraps, like all brothers and sisters. When we did, Olive often got at me by saying, "You're Daddy's favorite, and you get away with things."

"You're Mama's!" I really believed those words. One reason I insisted that Mama favored Olive was due to an incident when I was only seven or eight. We both had chores to do every day. Since we lived on the farm, I had to feed the chickens and bring in wood. Olive's chores included slopping the hogs.

One evening, Mama said, "Velma, go give Olive a hand with the hogs."

I didn't argue with Mama, but I didn't like it either. I took it out on Olive and started fussing and moaning. "Why do I have to help you? You never help me!" The words between us flew back and forth, and we accused each other of being the favorite.

We heard a noise and looked up. We saw Mama come

rushing out of the house and down toward the hogpen. She whipped us both with a rolling pin. I was wearing a dress, and the whipping left streaks on my legs.

Since Olive was wearing pants, the streaks didn't show. In reality, I doubt that she hit me harder, but that day I thought she had. "See, look at these marks on my legs. That shows she hit me harder." I believed she whipped me harder—every time—than she whipped Olive.

Years later I told a friend, "The hardest thing I can think of is for a child to grow up, not knowing she's loved."

4.

FOR WANT OF LOVE

When I was in first grade, I had a teacher I liked very much, and I worked hard to please her. I always liked school. For one thing, when I went to school I could forget about my home life.

I hated everything about my home life, but I kept it all inside. While I never stopped thinking about the things that troubled me, I had no one to talk to, so I learned to push away the pain and anger and to accept the situation. That's the way life is, I told myself.

I got used to doing a lot of work around the house. By the age of eleven or twelve, it seemed like I did almost everything. I didn't, but both Daddy and Mama put a heavy load on me. By the time I was eleven I knew how to keep house, wash and iron clothes, cook, mend, and take care of everything. By the time I was twelve, I was cooking practically all of the meals. When I reached fourteen, I had to take over the washing for a family of eleven people.

Daddy came to school on wash days about lunchtime and called me out of class to do the washing. We didn't have a machine, and so I had to do it all on a washboard, which took the rest of the day. It happened just about every week that he came and pulled me out of school. I resented being called out. A lot of those times I wanted to talk to somebody about all the bad feelings going on inside me, like all the resentment and anger over having to do so much work. I never did talk to

31

anyone else because I didn't know who would listen. And I didn't know who could do anything about it, anyhow. I just kept pushing everything deeper inside.

Probably the worst anger I felt toward both my parents came about because of something exciting at school. I had been chosen to play on the basketball team and I wanted to do it. Nobody had ever asked me to do anything before, and it made me feel special.

But instead of being happy for me, Mama said, "You got too much work to do at home."

"I'll still get my chores done," I protested. But I might as well have kept quiet. The team practiced after school. Daddy and Mama wouldn't let me stay after school for anything. Mama especially got mad if I dawdled a little on the way home.

"Too much to do," Mama said, "I need you here." That ended it. "I need you here."

I walked outside the house and I cried. Being on the team had meant so much to me. Not that I liked basketball all that much, but I wanted to do things with others at school and to be like other kids. I had gone into the house excited and happy. She had hardly listened to me, and I wondered then if she ever listened—really listened—to anything I said.

Later, I dried my face and tried to forget about playing basketball.

We didn't have much religious teaching at home, but we knew about the Bible and church and God. Even though we didn't always go to church, we knew how to sound like we were some of the best Christians around. Everybody quoted Bible verses, or parts of them, and we all knew the gospel songs.

We went twice each summer to the Presbyterian Bible school. Occasionally churches held what we called revivals. Those became big events in our rural communities, and we all liked to go because of the singing. When any of the churches around Parkton had revivals, my aunt nearly always went and sometimes she took us with her. She didn't attend church regularly herself—it was a kind of hit-and-miss thing—but, like the rest of us, she sure liked the singing.

Near where we lived, we had a holiness church, the Church of God. Sometimes Mama and Daddy went there if they had a hymn sing or a revival.

One time we started attending the Church of God. For two or three months we went every Sunday, then we quit as quickly as we had started. I don't remember why we stopped attending. As a family we didn't go anywhere again on any kind of regular basis.

When I was a teenager, though, I started regularly attending the Baptist church where all my friends went. When I turned sixteen, I joined the church and even got baptized. The day after my baptism, I told Daddy about it.

"You had no right to do that without asking me!" He got angry and yelled. I hadn't thought about his being upset. But then, I never knew what would upset him.

"You joined because of that Thomas Burke, didn't you?"

"No, Daddy, I didn't."

It didn't matter what I said, he believed that because Thomas and his family went there, I had joined just to be near him. Thomas and I had started dating, but I didn't join the church because of him.

I joined because it seemed the thing to do. My girl friends from school joined; most of them had even done it earlier.

For some reason, Daddy had never liked Thomas, and so I tried not to say much about him around home. Thomas and I had met when I was thirteen and we had barely moved to the Parkton area. I had just begun to notice boys, and when I met him, I thought he was one of the handsomest boys I had ever seen. He was a year older than me, and when he began to pay me a little attention, I felt like it was my first real chance to forget life at home. Thomas had a nice smile and even more than that, he was witty. He loved to joke a lot. I thought he had the most wonderful personality of any boy I had ever known. I've always been shy and didn't know how to mix very well with people. With Thomas around, I had a lot of fun. People liked Thomas and enjoyed laughing with him.

Being around Thomas made me feel like I was as good as other people and that I belonged.

Thomas liked me from the beginning, and he had all kinds of little ways to make me know he cared. No one had ever treated me so nicely before. From the time I was about fifteen or sixteen, I just basked in the sunshine of Thomas's love for me. He cared, and I needed someone to care for me.

I grew fond of Thomas because he treated me nicely and acted so patient with me. I found in Thomas what I had been searching for all along—somebody who would take time with me and really care.

Thomas and I started to go together when I was sixteen. Daddy wouldn't let me date anyone before then.

We didn't do much on a date. Thomas had an old car, and sometimes we would ride to the movies at Fayetteville. Sometimes we'd go to a barbecue place for a sandwich. Other times we just went for a drive.

As much as I liked being with Thomas and going places with him, I was bothered by thoughts that I should be home instead. Sometimes I couldn't even enjoy watching a movie because that anxious voice inside kept saying again and again, *It's getting late. You have a lot of things to do before you can go to bed. Why did you come here anyway?*

Mostly Thomas and I did simple things because we didn't have anything else to do. I didn't like inviting him over to our house. Even in the living room, I couldn't be sure we could sit and talk.

When Thomas and I were dating, Daddy changed over to the midnight shift. In the evenings, Daddy often slept in a room next to the living room. That meant we couldn't stay at the house because it might disturb Daddy. We worked it out so that Thomas came by the house, picked me up, and we went someplace else, even if only for a ride. Many evenings we drove around, talking mostly. I knew Thomas cared a lot about me because he told me often.

After we'd been going together about a year, we went to a movie in Fayetteville. I don't remember the name of it, but it had to do with a man and woman falling in love. They got married just before the end of the picture.

When we got into the car and started back toward Parkton, Thomas didn't say a lot at first. He mentioned that he liked the movie but then drove in silence for two or three miles.

When Thomas spoke again, he surprised me. "Velma, let's get married. What do you say?"

That's the way Thomas behaved, always saying things in a fun sort of way, but I knew he meant it.

"My daddy would never permit it."

"I want to marry you, Velma. I love you."

"You know Daddy," I said. I felt suddenly frightened because Daddy would never agree to our getting married. "Let's talk about it again later," I said.

"But I love you. I mean that."

"I know, Thomas. Let me think about it."

For the next day or so, I thought about it a lot. Maybe I finally convinced myself that I loved Thomas. Maybe I would have ended up marrying anyone who wanted to take me away from home. I only know that the more I thought about marrying Thomas, the better it sounded.

Two nights later, Thomas came by and picked me up. After we had driven away from my house I said, "Thomas, you remember what you asked me about a couple of nights ago?"

"Of course I remember."

"I can't just leave home and get married. My folks wouldn't let me. But you know something else? Daddy's decided to move up to Wade. That means I won't get to see you all the time."

"Then let's get married right away. Before your daddy leaves. Let's just elope."

"I guess that's the only way you and I can get married, isn't it?"

As we talked, I made my decision. If I hadn't been sure of how I felt about Thomas, moving out of town and going to a different school made me realize I didn't want to lose him.

We made our plans. We decided to run away and to get

married in South Carolina. I was seventeen and Thomas eighteen. He was a senior in high school, and I was a year behind him. By going across the state line to Dillon, South Carolina, we wouldn't have any trouble. Other couples had done it. We decided to elope and not tell our folks about it until Daddy got ready to move.

We figured that Daddy might get suspicious if Thomas picked me up and we were both dressed in our Sunday clothes. So Thomas asked his neighbor and friend, Alvie Pender, to come over and pick me up on the night of December 1, 1949.

My folks didn't like Thomas, but they liked Alvie. When Alvie came by, that seemed okay. Nobody even asked where we were going. Thomas met us a short way down the road, and the three of us drove over to Dillon. Alvie was our only witness.

It sounds a little funny the way we did it, but after the wedding, we drove back to Parkton. Thomas took me to my house and he went home to his. Because we had decided that we wouldn't say anything until my family got ready to move, it seemed safest to do what we did. We were both just two scared kids and needed time to figure out what to do next. We were still in school, although Thomas had already decided that he would quit if he had to.

Just like any other night, I went home and didn't say anything to anybody. I tried to keep on just like before, but it wasn't the same. The night after our wedding, Thomas picked me up, and we went to the movies. Afterward we talked a long time.

"We need to tell our folks," Thomas said.

"They'll find out sooner or later," I agreed. But I didn't want to tell them because I knew they would get mad. And that scared me.

"But I want them to know," Thomas said. "I love you, Velma, and I want us to live together, like it's supposed to be."

We talked until long after midnight. I knew Thomas was right, but I still didn't want to tell my parents. Thomas finally persuaded me that the longer I waited, the harder it would be because the pressure would keep building up. And the mad-der they might get, too.

"Okay, I'll tell them. Tonight," I promised. I was so scared, but I knew it had to be done.

When Thomas left me off, I went into the house and tried to think of how I could say it. It was past midnight. Daddy had gone to work on the third shift.

I finally sat down in a chair across from Mama. She had gone to bed, but had not fallen asleep. She usually stayed awake until every one of us had gotten home and into bed.

"Mama, I got to tell you something."

"What's that?" She raised up in bed, waiting for me to tell her what seemed so important.

"Last night," I began, "you know, Alvie came by to pick me up—but—but, well, I didn't go out with Alvie." Once I got started, I told her everything.

She stared at me while I finished telling her. In the rush of my excitement, I suppose I had hoped she would be excited, too.

But when I finally paused, instead of saying anything about Thomas or me, she said, "You'll have to tell your daddy."

"Why don't you tell him?"

She shook her head. "You got married. You have to tell him."

I didn't think much about it then, but Daddy scared her, too. She didn't want him screaming at her or hurting her, I suppose.

"Mama, please—"

"Now you say please. Maybe you should have said please yesterday. So, Velma, when your daddy gets in, you can tell him everything yourself."

I didn't argue because I knew it wouldn't do any good. And she was right. I had to tell Daddy myself.

I went on to bed, but I couldn't go to sleep right away. I kept thinking how nice it would be when Thomas and I had our own place. We planned to live with his folks for awhile. I liked the Burkes okay, and they liked me. Thomas said we'd have our own room. I'd be away from Daddy and Mama and from all the kids and the noise. If I had been totally honest with myself, I would have admitted I married Thomas mainly to get away from home. I was honest enough to know that I didn't love him the way I should—the way I wanted to care for a man—but I thought that would come in time.

The next morning I got up as usual. I didn't say a word to anybody about Thomas and me. Mama didn't mention what I had told her the night before. I sat around and waited until Daddy got in about 8:30.

Olive had quit school in the sixth grade so he could do the farmwork. By this time, he had gone to work at the same plant as Daddy. They worked the same shift, and so he and Daddy drove home together.

Daddy walked into the house and headed back for the bedroom. I stopped him because I had to tell him before he went to sleep.

"Daddy—Daddy, wait. I—I got something to tell you."

He stopped and turned around. I kept hoping that somehow he had already found out so that I wouldn't have to say anything. I didn't dare look at him when I said, "Two—two nights ago—well, two nights ago I went out and got married—"

"Got married? To Alvie?"

I shook my head. "No, to Thomas."

"Thomas Burke?" Daddy started yelling at the top of his voice. He grabbed a chair and threw it across the room. The chair didn't break, but it sounded like it ought to have. He kept yelling at me and saying things like, "I knowed that boy was no good! Why didn't you tell me?"

The tears streamed down my face. He had acted about the way I had expected. I had told him like I'd promised Thomas. Now he knew, and he just got madder and madder. "You got married!" He kept saying that over and over. "So you went out and got married, did you?"

Even though I had already told him, he asked me, "Who did you get married to?"

"Thomas." I explained about Alvie coming by to pick me up in case anybody suspected something.

"I'm going to have it annulled."

"No, Daddy!"

"Don't tell me no! We're going over to South Carolina right now and get that thing annulled, you hear me?"

The tears really came then, and they couldn't stop. I didn't try to argue with him—I could never argue with Daddy. I was so scared that I didn't know what to do. I thought for a minute he was going to hurt me really bad the way he had done Olive the time he whipped him until he started to bleed. But Daddy didn't touch me. He just kept yelling and throwing things.

"Olive!" he screamed. "You get dressed up and get ready to go to South Carolina. We're going to annul this thing."

Olive just stood there, staring at Daddy, not knowing what he was talking about.

"Just get dressed because we're going to hop into the car and go to South Carolina and get this marriage of your sister's annulled."

He started to yell at Olive as if he had done something wrong. Daddy was so angry that he started yelling at everybody.

After Olive got dressed, he walked out toward the car. Daddy came up close to him. "You knowed all about this thing of her getting married to Thomas."

Olive hadn't known, and no one else had either except Alvie. I tried to tell that to Daddy several times.

"I didn't know anything about her getting married until just right now!" I saw anger in Olive's eyes. He'd never talked back to Daddy like that.

"Don't lie to me! You knew all about this!"

Olive didn't yell, but the anger showed all right. "I didn't know anything about anybody getting married." Olive started to get into the car but he stopped. For a few seconds he just stared at Daddy. "And you ain't going to beat me anymore either!"

That must have taken all his courage to say those words because Olive took off running. We had a wooded area right in front of where we lived and he ran right for it, trying to get away from Daddy.

I hadn't said anything during all of that time he yelled at Olive. I couldn't do anything except cry. Every time I tried to stop, the tears would just come again. I felt helpless.

I don't think Mama cried, but then, I don't think I ever saw her cry much. She wasn't the kind of woman who expressed her feelings. Maybe she never knew how.

I expected to see Daddy go chasing Olive or at least yell at him, but he didn't do either. He stood there for a moment, with the most pitiful look on his face. Suddenly he slammed the other door of the car shut and walked back into the house.

I followed him, afraid to say anything and not knowing what to do. He went into the living room and picked up the chair he had thrown against the wall. He sat down in it. Then he did something I had never seen my daddy do before. He put his head down, cupped his chin with his hands, and began to cry.

I had never seen him weep like that. Even when his brother had died, he had only teared up a little. That's the only other time I remember seeing him cry. Even though losing his brother had disturbed him, this seemed to go deeper.

I felt even worse then because I was the cause of all the problems. *That's the way it always seems to work. No matter what I do, I do everything wrong. And now Daddy's hurt. I wish Thomas and I hadn't gotten married.* I felt guilty.

Daddy had raped me, had hurt me in hundreds of ways, but the thoughts going through my mind were about how much I had hurt him and let him down. Watching him cry made me feel as if I had robbed him of the joy of seeing me get married. I had failed again, as I always did in every part of my life. I couldn't seem to do anything right.

After a long time, Daddy stopped crying and went on to sleep in Olive's bed. He often slept there during the day. I didn't see him again until late that afternoon when he walked into the living room. "Where are you spending the night?" he asked.

"Thought I'd stay here for a night or two if you'll let me. After that we're going to start staying at Thomas's folks."

"All right," he said. He started getting ready for work.

He didn't seem to want to talk about it anymore. I worried that he might go into another tirade when he came home from work the next day, but he didn't. The issue was settled. He never brought up the matter of annulment again.

I stayed for a few more days, and on Saturday Thomas came by with his car. We moved my things, mostly clothes and not too many of them.

Oddly enough, after the night when I told Daddy about my getting married, he wasn't mean to me ever again. Until the day he died, he never threatened me again. He was like a different man.

But when I left my parents' home, I didn't think about Daddy being mean or not. Mostly I kept thinking about all the hurt and pain I had caused everybody.

Is that all I'm ever going to do? Cause hurt and pain to everyone?

5.

THE FIRST TRANQUILIZER

The happiest years of my life began with my marriage to Thomas Burke. He was patient and kind—nicer than anyone had ever been to me before.

When we married, Thomas quit school and went to work at a textile mill in Red Springs. We stayed with his parents for most of 1950. During the summer of 1951, Thomas quit his job and we moved to Wade, near my parents. For about a month he didn't have a job, and then he started working as a salesman for a soft drink company.

While I couldn't say I was happy every moment, life had changed for me. Even Daddy and Mama treated me better.

On December 12, 1951, I gave birth to a son, Ronald. Not quite two years later, on September 3, 1953, I had a daughter, Kim. I loved my children. Somewhere in those first two or three years, I learned to love my husband.

After Ronnie's birth we moved back to Parkton and rented the little house that my folks had rented at the time Thomas and I married. We stayed there until Ronnie entered the fifth grade. After that we moved into another rented house for awhile. Thomas's mother gave us an acre of land right outside Parkton, and Thomas built us a three-bedroom house.

When I left home and we moved in with Thomas's parents, we attended the Baptist church in Parkton with his mother. Thomas's father didn't go often, and I didn't go regu-

42

larly until Ronnie was about two years old. After that, I took both kids to Sunday school and church every week.

Until both kids graduated from high school, I attended and was involved in all kinds of church activities. At one time I even taught Sunday school. If you had asked me what I believed, I could have given the kind of answers everybody gave because I knew how to use the same words everybody else around the church used. I would have said something like, "I believe in Jesus Christ as my Savior." Like everybody else, I knew the right words. I had a vague kind of understanding of God, and I always believed in God. While I didn't discuss it with anyone, I didn't think God liked me—how could He? And while I prayed and did whatever everyone else did, I knew deep inside that I wasn't good enough for God to care about.

One day in the mid-1950s I was standing in my yard. I had been to a basketball game with Mama and Daddy. Thomas had stayed home and kept Kim who was only about three. Ronnie, nearly five, was old enough to enjoy part of the game, and so I had taken him with us.

Daddy pulled off the road to let us out of the car. He heard a car coming from the opposite direction. The driver of the other car, as we learned later, thought Daddy was on his side of the road. It was late at night, foggy, and the man headed right for the ditch. When he got to the corner of the yard, and realized what he had done, he tried to steer his car back onto the road. But he had been drinking and couldn't react quickly enough.

I heard the car when it left the shoulder, but it didn't sink in. My mother had rolled down the window and was talking to me about the wedding plans of one of my younger brothers.

Suddenly I heard the car and saw its headlights coming toward me. I started to run but was a little too late. The car struck me. I hardly felt the impact because the fender merely grazed me enough to knock me off balance. When I fell, I turned my ankle.

I tried to get up, but I couldn't stand on my feet. I lay back down on the ground. By that time, Daddy was out of his car and kneeling down beside me. Thomas had heard the car horn blowing—apparently the panicked man had pressed on the horn when he saw me. Thomas came running outside.

Daddy ran into the house and called the doctor. The doctor said, "Get her off the damp ground and into the house." Thomas and Daddy lifted me up and helped me inside.

I was sure it was only a bad sprain. The doctor came by and gave me a shot for the pain and said, "See me tomorrow morning at 8:00." I was in pain all night. By morning, the pain was worse, and my whole leg was swollen. I went to the doctor's office, and the doctor sent me to the hospital. X-rays showed that the ankle was broken and that surgery would be necessary. I stayed in the hospital twelve days.

The doctor prescribed a strong analgesic which relieved the pain. I had to rest a lot and stay in traction most of the time so that the bones would set properly.

I went through my first real period of depression in the hospital. I felt awful most of the time, even though the shots took care of the pain. I kept thinking of my two children at home and my not being able to take care of them. I lay in the hospital bed and cried. I couldn't seem to stop. I'd feel all right, and then someone would visit and the least little thing would start me crying again. I wanted to be alone, and I kept the room dark. It seemed to me that either I cried all through the night or else I slept. I suppose the nurses thought I cried from my physical pain. It was something much deeper.

When I finally went home I was overjoyed to see the children. My depression didn't fully leave, but I got better. Since I had no idea of what depression was and couldn't figure out what made me feel weepy, we blamed it on the aftereffects of surgery.

I lost my energy about that time, and nothing mattered anymore. I had always tried to keep the house spotless, but I could look at dirt and shrug it off. Or I'd think, *I ought to clean up this place.* I didn't want to go out and didn't want to be with people as I had before.

I started to work when Ronnie entered the first grade. Thomas's mother kept the kids after school and on vacation days. At one time I worked at a textile mill in Raeford. That job put me on the midnight-to-eight shift. My hours made it pretty hard for Thomas and me to see much of each other, because he worked days. I made sure I was there when he came home, and I didn't go to bed in the mornings until after he left. Looking back, I've wondered if that's when our problems together really began.

My health wasn't too good. In 1962, when I was thirty years old, I had a hysterectomy. I had been hemorrhaging and was feeling tired all the time. The doctor scheduled me for surgery to remove my uterus and ovaries. I never felt I really needed that surgery, but I agreed to it. I didn't want any more babies, and that was one more reason for me to have the surgery.

After that surgery, and especially by 1963, I found myself tensing up all the time. I asked the doctor who had operated on me if the problem with my nerves could be on account of the surgery. He said it could and added, "These things happen sometimes, especially when the woman is as young as you are."

That surgery had a bad effect on me because I didn't know how to handle my nerves. From my early childhood, when anything upset me it made me nervous and afraid. All of that got worse after my hysterectomy. I had hidden my feelings and kept so much inside me that it built up over the years. As I got older I still didn't know how to do anything about the anger and the guilt. I didn't know anyone that I could walk up to and say, "Listen, let me talk to you about this."

Some time during the 1960s Thomas began to drink. I don't remember the year, but as I've tried to trace it back, I would say about 1965.

I can think of three things that might have either caused or influenced his drinking. One might have been the death of his father. After Mr. Burke died, Thomas took it hard but didn't talk about it a lot.

Thomas also had been involved in a car accident, and for

months after that he complained about headaches. Maybe he drank to get rid of the pain—but he never told me that.

The last reason—and the one I think had the most influence—was that by 1965 Thomas had joined a civic organization and had begun to drink regularly. Up until then, he had an occasional drink, maybe even two, but no more than that. Nobody twisted his arm, but those other men influenced him. He quit his job and went to work delivering and selling for a rival soft drink company, and later another. He did a good job and said he liked his work. However, sometimes after working hours, he stopped for a drink with some of his friends. When he went to meetings or any place with his new friends, he drank heavily. His drinking got worse.

The group sponsored dances and things like that—events with liquor available. Thomas put his heart into the organization and spent more and more time with the members.

By 1966 he drank regularly and heavily. As Thomas started to drink more, his whole personality changed. What had happened to the patient man I had learned to love? I couldn't tolerate the change that had come over him. Daddy had acted the same way when he drank.

I became impatient with Thomas and argued with him about his drinking. That didn't do any good, and I suppose I never thought about that. In my anger and frustration, I kept at him about his drinking. He seemed to keep on increasing the amount and the frequency. I couldn't stand to live with a man who drank like that.

The children and I were scared when he drank. He never hurt any of us, but we were afraid that he would. We had had so much good in the first years of our marriage that I couldn't accept the difference.

When he came home after a lot of drinking, he would spill things, push over chairs, the table, anything. His language got coarse—not like the old Thomas.

Only one time did he ever actually hit me. I can't recall everything that happened, but we were arguing about his drinking. Thomas went into a rage and struck me. I pushed him away and he fell to the floor. I ran next door to his mother's house.

We never stopped arguing over things, and I finally decided he had become an alcoholic, because he couldn't leave liquor alone. I don't think Thomas ever realized how it had a hold on him—at least he never acknowledged it to me. He denied how much or how often he drank, and he would say that he could quit if he wanted to.

When I challenged him to quit, he started on me by telling me things like, "If you made it a little more nice to come home, I'd probably come home more often and drink a lot less."

I had a lot of guilt over that, too. As I look back, it didn't take much for me to feel guilty about anything. I felt guilty because I couldn't be more patient with him. "I can't tolerate this," I said to him and to myself. Then an inner part of me would seem to whisper, *If you were the right kind of wife you would understand. You wouldn't nag him all the time.*

He began coming home every afternoon so loaded with drink that he could hardly walk. I was afraid he would wreck the car and even kill himself one evening. I finally talked with two doctors about help for Thomas. Both said he should be hospitalized at Dorothea Dix State Hospital.

One Monday evening when he was drunk, a sheriff's deputy—acting on papers I had signed earlier—picked him up and drove him to the hospital. He checked himself out three days later.

"Don't you ever do that to me again!" he yelled. For several days he wouldn't talk to me.

I don't think Thomas ever forgave me for having him hospitalized. He had a certain amount of pride, and I had embarrassed him in front of the whole world. I had no idea that it would affect him so deeply. And, again, even though I had done it to help, I ended up feeling guilty for having had him committed. *Wrong again.*

Often days passed without much talking going on between us. In some ways the silence sounded worse than the arguing and fighting.

Thomas's drinking got so bad that the next day after a bout he would stay in bed because he felt so miserable.

His boss didn't want to let Thomas go, but he didn't know

what to do. Twice he came to see me, hoping I could figure
out a way to stop his drinking—at least on the job. Once he
even talked to Ronnie. I felt bad about that, laying a heavy
burden on Ronnie, because he had no idea how to help.

Thomas lost his job around 1966. He had liked that job.
The police ticketed him for driving under the influence, and
he lost his license. With no license, he couldn't hold his job
because it required driving much of the time.

That was a low point for Thomas. He stopped caring—or
that's the way it seemed to me. He didn't seem to mind that he
didn't have a job.

The burden fell on me to take care of the family. I had been
working for years, but at one time things got so bad that I
held down two jobs. I worked days as a clerk in a department
store in Fayetteville and nights as a machine operator in a cotton mill in Hope Mills.

I didn't sleep enough, and I felt tired all the time. But we
had to have food and clothes.

When the kids were born, Thomas was the most loving father any man could be. He was always so concerned about
the children when they were small that he didn't want them
out of his sight.

But by the summer of 1968, he had changed. Thomas had
gone somewhere with his friends and had come home drunk
one Friday afternoon. He continued to drink on Saturday.
Ordinarily I worked Saturdays, but I was off on that particular day. I was inside, cleaning up the house, when I heard
Ronnie's scream.

"Daddy! Daddy! Don't do that!"

I ran outside and saw them under the carport. Thomas had
Ronnie backed up against the house. He held a knife with the
blade against Ronnie's chest.

Hurting Ronnie is one of the last things Thomas—the old
Thomas—would have done. I ran between them and pushed
the knife away. I screamed something like, "Are you crazy?"

Ronnie was nearly seventeen and as tall as his dad. He
could easily have defended himself, but he would not have
touched his father.

Thomas put the knife away and walked into the house. He never said a word.

I don't know of anything like that ever happening again, but it made me know that when my husband began drinking, he could be as bad as my father had been to us kids.

Thomas began to do strange things that scared all of us, especially the children. They never wanted to ride anywhere with him because they were afraid he might crash into a wall or run off the highway. Many times he sat in his car in the driveway and raced the engine, making terrible noises. That scared the kids, making them ask, "What is Daddy trying to do?"

Some time in that same year, 1968, I collapsed. I had gotten up one Sunday morning to cook breakfast. Ronnie was in the kitchen when I came down. I started to walk toward the refrigerator when everything went black. I passed out and fell to the floor.

It scared Ronnie and he got on the phone and called Daddy immediately. Thomas had been drinking too much to help. By the time Daddy got there, I had come to. I sat up and looked around, not understanding what had happened. I felt confused. "What am I doing on the floor?"

"You just fell down, Mama."

I wondered what had caused that. Because I didn't know, it scared me.

My passing out concerned Daddy, and he insisted on taking me to the hospital. He drove me to the emergency room at a hospital in Fayetteville.

On the way to the hospital, I burst into tears and couldn't stop. I couldn't even talk to explain. Even if I could have said anything, I don't know what it would have been. Not only could I not stop crying, I didn't know what made me cry. That confused me all the more.

The doctor asked me questions, and I couldn't answer him because as soon as I tried to say anything, new spasms of crying started.

"I think we ought to admit her," the doctor said. "Let's keep her over the weekend. On Monday her regular doctor can take a look at her."

On Monday when my doctor came in, I still couldn't talk to anyone. As soon as I tried to say anything, I started crying again. He left then. That same evening he came back, and I had calmed down. He talked to me a while and asked a lot of questions. Finally he said, "You've had a nervous break-down."

He said a lot of other things, but I couldn't really concentrate because I couldn't stop crying for more than a few minutes at a time. As soon as I tried to speak or someone said anything, new waves of tears came.

"You've been under a lot of stress," he said. "We'll do what we can to alleviate some of that."

I had no awareness of how bad the stress had become. But as I lay in the hospital bed and reviewed the events of the past year, it helped to explain what had happened to me.

"I want to keep you here a few more days," he said, "and build you up." He ordered lots of fluids. I also received lots of medication.

So far as I know, that was the first time I ever received a tranquilizer.

6.

APRIL 19, 1969

The doctor kept me in the hospital for a week and it did me a world of good. With shots of iron and vitamin B, tranquilizers, and whatever other medication he gave me, I rested. I went home feeling better than I had in a long time.

The doctor gave me a prescription for tranquilizers, telling me, "I want you to take one every day."

I didn't follow his directions. I started taking a capsule only as I felt I needed it. For the first few months, I didn't take more than half a dozen.

It occurred to me that the medication helped only if I took it according to the doctor's instructions. I decided to take it regularly. Taking a capsule a day, I found I could cope better with hectic situations. I did it just as the doctor said, one capsule every morning. Whatever the medication did for me, I know my nerves improved, and I felt less edgy. I wondered why I had resisted his orders.

One day the pressures bore down on me so heavily that I didn't think I could make it. I remembered my collapse and having to stay at the hospital. I didn't want anything like that again. That particular morning everything had started off wrong and I felt more nervous than usual. Simple questions confused me, making me wonder if I was losing my mind.

I went to my medicine cabinet and took out a second capsule. Minutes after taking it, the nervousness disappeared, and my mind cleared. I had not intended to take that second capsule, but I had to do something. I promised myself, "Just this time."

The next day I repeated the double dosage again, telling myself, "Just until I get past all of this pressure, and Thomas gets straightened out a little."

After a few weeks, I regularly swallowed two, and sometimes three, a day. Then it became a ritual of two or three, twice or three times in a single day. "Just until I can get past all this stress," I kept telling my guilty conscience, "then I'll cut all the pills out. But right now I need this medication."

By the time I regularly doubled (or tripled), I ran into a real problem. The doctor had prescribed only so much medication, and I was running out before I should. After thinking about it awhile, I went to another doctor, and he gave me a prescription, too. That way I could have heavier doses and not worry about running out.

During the time that I increased my medication, Thomas lost his job. Fortunately I still worked, so we had my check coming in. Eventually Thomas found a job at the mill where he had worked when we were first married. Having to go back was a real blow to his pride, and he seemed to drink even more.

I kept thinking that everything would ease up. *Thomas has a job again and he'll pull out of this when he sees what he's doing to himself. Then I'll stop feeling so nervous all the time and can begin to cut down on the medication.*

Nothing eased for me. Thomas's drinking got worse, and I felt guilty for not being more patient with him. I seemed to fight depression all the time. By then, I understood depression. I kept worrying that I had pushed Thomas into heavier drinking because of my impatience.

My first doctor suffered a heart attack and moved away. I still had several refills on his prescription which I used. His leaving meant I had to start seeing another doctor. That didn't present any problem, only the added expense of office calls. The new doctor gave me a prescription for Butisol sedative. It wasn't long before he also prescribed Librium, Valium, and other pills.

I started getting occasional headaches. Their frequency increased after a while, and so did their intensity. Blinding pain would lash across my temples. At first I tried aspirin, but the headaches wouldn't go away. I went to still another doctor and got prescriptions for tranquilizers, sleeping pills, and pills for headaches.

It got to be the same every time I visited a doctor, whether for the first or the fifth time. I talked a few minutes and ended up with prescriptions for tranquilizers and muscle relaxants, mostly Valium, and sleeping pills. Sometimes the medication also included analgesics.

The pills worked, but only temporarily. As long as I kept taking my medication I would be all right. I know now that my real hurting was inner pain and the medication only masked it for a few hours. The effects always wore off, and so I had to take more to get free of the pressures and guilt. While under the heavy medication I didn't feel so guilty because I didn't feel much of anything. I didn't have to think or worry. I moved through life without feeling really good, but I never felt really awful either.

People may have suspected I was on medication, but for a long time no one said anything to me. Once or twice I mentioned that the doctor had given me something because of my bad nerves. Three of the ladies I worked with knew of my medication and so did my manager—but none of them knew how much. By that point, I didn't either.

Thomas started working the midnight shift at the mill as a slasher/tender. He got off work at 8:00 A.M., but some days he didn't get home until 10:00. On April 19, 1969, Thomas came home late. Without having to ask, I knew he had stopped for drinks. He was showing the effects of it. His speech was slurred, and he could hardly stand up.

I don't know clearly what happened that morning because I blanked it from my mind for so many years. The anger in me had built up against Thomas. He had been so good in the beginning of our marriage—now he could hardly keep the same job where he had started twenty years earlier.

That morning when he half stumbled into the house, I said to myself, *I can't take this any longer! I can't stand any more!* I took extra medication, wanting something to stop the burning anger in my heart. After he had been in the house a few minutes, he nodded off to sleep while sitting in a chair smoking. The cigarette fell out of his mouth, rolled onto his shirt, and if I hadn't grabbed it, he would have set himself on fire.

As I picked up the burning cigarette and put it out, I screamed, "I don't care! I don't care anymore! Burn yourself up if you want to!"

Thomas roused himself enough to drag himself to the bedroom and fall down on the bed. He didn't bother to undress.

His drunkenness had become commonplace. I got into my car and picked up my niece. We drove over to Mama's, picked her up, and we took our clothes to a washateria.

My niece and I came back to the house two hours later. I parked the car and went inside the house. I smelled smoke. I ran into the room where Thomas had been. The smoke was so thick that I couldn't see him. I ran outside screaming. Frances, Thomas's sister, was passing by in her car.

"Frances! Call the fire department!"

I don't remember if she jumped out of the car and ran next door to her mother's house or if she drove to the fire department and rescue unit since it was located just around the corner. Both the fire and rescue people arrived within minutes.

The fire fighters made me stay outside while they went into the house and back to the bedroom. They hadn't been inside long before one of them ran back out and then hurried back inside carrying a stretcher. Less than a minute later, they carried Thomas out.

"How is he? What's wrong?" I kept begging, but they wouldn't tell me anything. Inside, I knew he was already dead.

One of the fire fighters later told me, "It appears that he was lying in bed and that he fell asleep smoking. He must have dropped the lighted cigarette." The man thought that the smell of smoke in the room must have awakened Thomas, that it looked as if he had stomped on the rug next to the bed trying to put out the fire. It was assumed that Thomas died from smoke inhalation.

On the way to the hospital, I picked up Kim and Ronnie. I didn't tell them much except that their father had been taken to the hospital and that I didn't know how bad he was.

When we arrived at the emergency room, a nurse made us wait in a small room for maybe fifteen minutes. The door opened, and the head nurse came in and told us that Thomas was already dead when they brought him into the hospital.

Both of the children broke into tears. Even though their father had been drinking heavily the last few years, they still loved him. I'm sure they also felt a lot of emptiness.

After I heard the words that Thomas was dead, I felt worse than I ever had before. Old feelings of guilt struck at me, stronger than ever. I don't remember if I burst into tears or exactly what I did, but the nurse did ask me a question, "Would you like us to give you something, Mrs. Burke?"

I nodded. I needed something—anything—to numb me, to help me forget what had taken place.

She gave me a shot to ease my grief. I didn't feel much of anything for several hours. The only way I knew to stop thinking and feeling was through medication.

Just enough to get me through today. I must have said it to myself dozens of times. That's how it went—taking just enough medication to make it through one more day, every day. I never stopped to think about it. As much as possible, I avoided thinking. After Thomas's death, it took every inner reserve I had, along with an increased dosage of medication, just to survive.

7.

ADDICTION

For the next year after Thomas's death, I existed. I can't think of any better way to say it. I took my pills before I did anything else in the mornings. My whole life revolved around getting refills and making sure I had enough medication to last me through the week.

I continued to work at the department store. It was the only reason I got up in the mornings. I knew I had to work. I had been at the store for several years when Thomas died. I enjoyed my job in housewares and linens, but as the days dragged by, I lost a little more interest each day. A lot of things were going on inside me—grieving over Thomas's death and trying to live with fear and guilt. I couldn't face it. I needed to escape. I increased my medication.

Pauline Barfield worked in the department next to mine, piece goods and linens. We had our lunch breaks at the same time, and so we got to know each other pretty well. We usually sat together in the lounge and talked. Other than the people I carpooled with, I probably knew her better than anyone else at the store. We never became close friends—I never made any close friends there—but I got as close to her as I did to anyone.

Once in awhile her husband would come to see her or to pick her up. She introduced Jennings to me and he made it a point to stop and talk to me for a few minutes whenever he came into the store.

Jennings had been forced to retire early because he suffered from emphysema. His condition was so serious that he kept an oxygen container in his bedroom. Jennings smoked a lot, which only made his condition worse. He was also diabetic and didn't watch his diet closely.

One day Pauline didn't come to work because she had scheduled a doctor's appointment in the morning. She suffered a cerebral hemorrhage that afternoon and was rushed to the hospital. She died a few hours later.

Her unexpected death shocked everyone since Jennings had been the sick one. I missed her, but that would have been the end of my relationship with the Barfields if Jennings hadn't come back to the store some months later. It was the early fall of 1969.

"How are you doing?" I asked. It was the first time I had seen him since the funeral.

"About the same, I guess. Just wanted to come by and see you. See how you're doing." He looked so lonely. It must have been hard on him to walk right past the part of the store where his wife had worked.

"I'm doing all right," I told him. We talked in a general kind of way for a few minutes.

When he got ready to leave he said, "Uh, Velma, I wondered if you'd like to have something to eat with me after work?"

"Sure," I said. "That'll be nice."

His taking me out to eat became the first of frequent invitations at the end of a workday. He was lonely and wanted a wife. Jennings Barfield was older than I was, but I was lonely too. I missed Thomas. The kids, now teenagers, didn't need me the way they had when they were younger. I was grateful that he wanted to take me out. It made me feel good.

For the next couple of months, Jennings came by the store regularly about the time I got off work, and we went out to eat. He was so sick that I don't think he had the strength to do much else.

One evening just as we finished our meal, Jennings asked me to marry him. "I need a good woman around, Velma, and you're a good woman."

I agreed to marry Jennings Barfield even though I wasn't in love with him. I knew that Jennings didn't drink and that he wouldn't treat me bad. I didn't think much about his needs. I just wanted someone to be with me and to talk to me. I wanted someone so badly to fill the emptiness in my life.

We were married on August 23, 1970. I don't know what I expected to happen, but marrying Jennings didn't change things much. I was as unhappy married as I had been alone.

I tried to take good care of him, but it was difficult. Sometimes, especially after he had been smoking, he had trouble breathing. More than once, he tried to get his oxygen set on but passed out before he could get it going. I'd have to rush him to the doctor's office.

He refused to follow his diet, and I became frustrated trying to keep him on it. Because he took his insulin shots every day, he thought he didn't have to eat what the doctor recommended. He said, "This takes care of that for me."

In the meantime I gradually increased my medication. In November, only three months after we married, I overdosed and ended up in the hospital's emergency room. Fortunately, I woke up by myself. They kept me overnight for observation and released me the next day.

I overdosed a second time three months later. The doctor had to give me oxygen to revive me.

The doctor on duty wanted to run a series of tests—spinal tap, brain scan, and psychiatric evaluations. He kept me in the hospital for a week and asked that another doctor come to see me. The second doctor talked with me in my hospital room and set up an appointment for me to come to his office.

During the hospital stay, neither doctor talked to me about the amount of medication I was taking or suggested that I had a drug problem. Neither of them even asked me why I took an overdose.

If they had asked me, I couldn't have given them an answer. I don't recall intentionally overdosing. I had become so erratic in my pill taking that I never seemed to take the same dosage two times in a row. My muddled mind couldn't reason out all those things about doses and aftereffects. Those capsules and pills were a way to get rid of persistent pain and burning anger.

I experienced some withdrawal pains in the hospital. The doctor had taken away all medication but the mildest tranquilizer. No matter how much I begged, he refused to give me anything strong.

The last time I saw the doctor who had admitted me was on a Friday. After he left my room, he went to the nurses' desk and told them to discharge me on Monday. He hadn't even told me. I think that all he wanted was to dry me out—detoxify me, as they said in the hospital units. He still had said nothing to me about my addiction. In those days, not much was done in the way of counseling. We were just supposed to survive our overdoses. During that whole week, I saw my other doctor three times. Once we were "okay," we went home.

Life with Jennings got worse. I not only had to cope with getting up and living each day, but I had the heavy responsibility of taking care of him. He stubbornly refused to follow his doctor's orders. The more obstinate he became, the more medicine I took. The more exasperated I grew, the more desperate I felt. *I wish I could be free of all this. I want to get away. Why did I marry him anyway? I was better off before I married him.*

Each day got worse. *I can't bear up under all of this. I've got to get away from this pressure. I can't stand it much longer.*

I bought a bottle of poison. *My God! What am I doing? Stop!* I was so confused. Part of me cried that it was the only way. Another part of me begged to stop. I was so confused. *This will make him sick. Then he'll be sorry he's caused me so much trouble, and he won't do it again. He'll start acting right, and he won't bother me anymore. It won't hurt him. He shouldn't be treating me so bad.*

That afternoon, Jennings had difficulty breathing, and he started vomiting. *He's sick. Oh my God, he's sick. I better get help.* I rushed Jennings to the hospital. It was a Sunday, I remember.

After he was admitted, a doctor called me out of the room.

"I can't give you much hope that Mr. Barfield will even make it through the night."

Jennings died at 10:30 the next morning.

After Jennings's death I felt emptier and more depressed than ever. I kept going to my doctors. I had prescriptions from at least two, and usually three, doctors at any time. At one period, I had prescriptions from four doctors. I used different drugstores so that no one would catch on.

I was addicted. No matter how many pills any one doctor prescribed, they never lasted until time for the next refill. I never had enough. It got so that I just called or went in to see a doctor and said what I needed. I had learned what I should say to get the medication I wanted. That's all there was to it.

I blanked out what I had done to cause Jennings's death. Whenever disturbing thoughts came to me, I reminded myself of his emphysema, aggravated by his smoking, and his diabetes. *He was in terrible health when I married him. I didn't cause his death. His lungs just gave out.*

I started missing work; I'd never done that before. I just didn't care about my job the way I had in the past. Nothing made sense to me. I wanted to care but couldn't. I had such a hurting inside and carried even more guilt than ever.

I overdosed again. It was different from before. I knew what I was doing. I was going to do away with myself. My attempted suicide was as much a failure as my attempted life. I ended up at the hospital and was kept for three weeks. I was put through more tests, but the staff said little to me. So far as I can remember, no one talked to me about my heavy medications or about any kind of addiction.

I functioned less and less, doing only the minimum around the house. When Jennings and I married, we had moved to a home in a neighboring town. I had rented out the house that Thomas had built. After Jennings's death, I went back to the house. It was Kim's last year of high school. She moved in with my parents in Parkton. That way she could finish out her senior year in the school where all her friends went.

I couldn't stand being back in that house. I redecorated and bought new furniture, but I didn't like living there. I tried, but I just couldn't feel good in it. Being in the house that Thomas had built made me think I was drowning and didn't know how to swim.

When Ronnie or Kim came around, I tried to conceal how bad I felt about the house. Ronnie's draft number was getting close, and it was right in the middle of the Vietnam conflict. He kept worrying and thinking about what he should do. He enlisted in the Army and was sent to Fort Jackson in South Carolina for basic training.

With Ronnie in the service and Kim with my parents, a lot of pressure was taken off me. But things still didn't change for me. I was depressed. I couldn't make myself *care* anymore. I stopped making mortgage payments because it took too much energy to think about writing out a check. I lost the house. I didn't care. Maybe I was even glad I lost it because I could never go back to live in that house again. Losing the house didn't solve anything, but I wasn't thinking clearly. It was easier just to increase my medicine and let the days come and go.

My supervisor at work finally came to me. As soon as he started talking, I knew what he was going to say. I had expected it for a long time. The store had put up with me long enough, maybe because I had been working there nearly seven years. Until the time of Thomas's death, I had been a dependable worker. It was late 1971.

"I'm sorry, Velma," he said. I knew it was hard on him to fire me.

I should have cried or done something, but I couldn't. My feelings were numbed by medication.

After losing my job I lay around the house, not doing much of anything. For a while I lived on the small amount of insurance money left after Jennings's death. I knew it wouldn't last forever, but I couldn't think about forever. I had enough problems trying to figure out how to survive until the next day.

My daddy had come down with laryngitis in the summer. He recovered but relapsed a short time later. Daddy went into the hospital for tests that fall. The doctors told him it resulted from his angina.

Daddy got worse and seemed sick all the time. I moved in with my parents. I lost a lot of weight and Mama finally said to me, "You look like you've lost thirty pounds." I probably had because I didn't stay up and eat. I slept as much as I could to escape from everything. One time I slept for almost a full week. I woke up, struggled out of bed, used the bathroom, took more medicine, and went on back to bed. I didn't want to stay awake. By sleeping so much, I didn't have to think about Jennings's or Thomas's deaths or Daddy's sickness or my guilt or anything else.

Daddy got steadily worse and looked awful. He kept losing weight, no matter how much he ate. He didn't have much appetite anyway, so that made it harder to get him to eat. Yet every morning, no matter how bad he felt, Daddy got dressed and came into the dining room-den combination. He had a regular chair he sat in. He didn't feel like doing much of anything, but he refused to stay in bed.

About that time Daddy had a real conversion experience, and he talked about what a difference God made in his life. He had become involved with a nearby Baptist church before he got sick, and his pastor came by and visited from time to time.

Daddy had already gone to several doctors and to the hospital, but nobody could explain or diagnose his problem. Additional tests were run at the hospital, and angina was still blamed. He left the hospital no better. His doctor made an appointment for him to check into a hospital in Winston-Salem in February of 1972 for thorough testing.

In late January, his pastor told him about a respiratory hospital. "Used to be some place where they only helped people with tuberculosis, but now it's also set up for people with certain types of breathing problems, even cancer—anything respiratory. You might be able to get some help over there."

Daddy hesitated because he was already scheduled to go into the other hospital the following month. "How do I know they'll do me any good?" he asked.

"Why don't you try to get into this special hospital? If you don't like it, you would still have time to keep your original appointment."

Daddy agreed to be admitted. Within a few days we learned the source of Daddy's problem.

The first doctor who saw him at the hospital, a man from the West Indies, took one look at him and said, "I think I know his problem."

"What is it?" we asked.

"I'm going to run some tests on him to be sure. As soon as I have the results, I shall let you know."

Two days later, Mama and I went to the hospital and talked to the doctor. He told us that his suspicions had been correct. "He has cancer of the lungs."

I can't remember all the conversation that followed. As soon as I heard the word *cancer*, nothing else registered.

"When do you think he'll be able to come home again?" Mama asked.

He shook his head. "He can never come home again. Not to stay."

I think he had been trying to tell us that for several minutes, but we finally understood.

I walked out of the hospital and one thing kept going over and over in my head: *Daddy is going to die.*

He stayed in the hospital sixty-six days, coming home only one time for about a week. He was so sick during that week, I don't know that it did him any good. We took him back to the hospital. We visited him regularly. Everytime we went, we could see him going downhill fast.

As Daddy got worse, I got worse. *What can possibly matter anymore? Nothing.* I kept myself medicated as much as I could because I didn't want to think about his dying. I didn't want to think about anything.

Daddy died in April.

Two months earlier, I had gotten a job with a knitting plant in Raeford. I worked there during March and in April until Daddy died. After Daddy's death, I didn't want to go back. I went over to the textile mill in Raeford where I had worked years earlier when the kids were small. I got a job back in the same department as a twister tender. I worked hard for three months and had even begun to figure out how I could cut down on my medication. Then indifference set in again, and I lost the desire to change. Maybe it was depression. Maybe it was simply a natural effect from taking so much medication for so long.

I might have stayed longer except for my medication. Every morning I took my medication before I left for work. Sometimes I took a small pick-me-up in the middle of the day.

On one occasion, I had taken a little too much during the day. When my carpool driver stopped in front of Mama's house to let me out, I just fell out and lay on the ground, passed out. The lady ran to the house and got my mother. Ronnie must have been visiting because between Ronnie and the two women, they got me into the house.

Ronnie called the Lumberton hospital, and he was told to bring me in. I was examined, tested, and kept for two weeks.

Once out of the hospital, I found a new job at a department store in Red Springs. The pattern began to repeat itself. I'd find a job, get heavily involved in it for a month or so, and then lose interest. By the end of the second month, or at most by the third, I had either quit or had been fired.

The best I can describe things in those days, I was like two different people. One "me" could function and do the assigned job. The other "me" didn't want to just function. She wanted to get out—to be a real person and to enjoy life. But she was trapped. I took more drugs to find relief, and the cycle kept going.

I wanted so much to talk to someone, to explain, to get help. But just as when I was a teenager, I didn't know how. If someone came into the same room, I wanted to run away and be alone. My feelings were mixed. As much as I wanted somebody to hear me, I didn't want to be near anyone.

8.

A RAGE UNLEASHED

I took a lot of pain killers and tranquilizers together. Some days I remember well. Some days I can recall only bits and parts. Others are blank because I was so far out of it. Even when I was aware of events going on around me, I didn't always understand what they meant. I find it hard to explain how it was. I could see and hear everything going on around me, but I was like an observer, not a participant. I functioned like a robot. I showed no emotions. I felt nothing. For days at a time, I neither felt pain nor happiness. Nothing. The emotional part of my life had been taken out and stored away.

I didn't go to work regularly for nearly three years. I would find a job, work at it a few weeks, leave it or get fired, and then do nothing. After a month of sitting around and sleeping, I'd start to run low on medication and be forced to work again.

I overdosed again and had to be taken to the hospital. When I was released, I moved in with Mama for a few weeks. That didn't work out, and so I rented a place of my own in Whiteville, North Carolina. I worked about three months in a textile plant there. I was miserable the whole time. I was so alone. No one in the family was near me.

In January 1973 I overdosed again. Somehow I ended up in the Whiteville hospital. My family told me later that the doctor came out into the hallway and talked with them.

"It doesn't look as if she's going to make it through this overdose."

I pulled through, though, and stayed in the hospital for a full week. After I was released, I was still miserable and unhappy. I couldn't pull myself together enough to go back to work, and so finally I did the only thing I knew to do. On February 7, 1973, I moved back to my mother's house. Mama was alone, and she had asked me several times to live with her. She had heart trouble and some problems with her nerves. She took two or three different kinds of medication each day.

I'm sure Mama meant it when she said she wanted me. But sometimes she said cruel things. When people came to visit, she'd warn them before they even sat down. "If you have any medicine in your purses, you'd better hide them real good because Velma will take any kind of pill she can find."

I tried not to let it show how much that hurt. But it made me wonder if she got pleasure out of embarrassing me. The months passed, but her painful comments didn't.

Mama liked to sit and talk about the old days when we were kids. She was getting old and maybe that's why she kept talking like that.

Almost every day she started on the same things again. I heard it over and over until I couldn't stand it anymore.

"I wish we could go back to when you were thirteen or fourteen again." She'd sigh, sometimes I even saw a tear in her eyes. "They was good days."

"Mama, forget the past. We can't go back—"

"But they was such good times. The best days I ever had in my life."

"They weren't my best days." She didn't listen to my objections. She never asked why I said that or asked anything about the way I felt.

"Mama! Please!" I pleaded.

Sometimes she started on me about my medications. "You're killing yourself, Velma. You can't keep on doing that."

"Mama, I get my medications from the doctors. They know I need this for my nerves."

Then she'd say, "Oh, if only it would be like it was when you was thirteen. You was such a good girl then."

Those constant references to the past brought back the old anger and guilt. Especially when she talked about those years as being happy ones, I remembered things like being called out of school, having to do the cooking, and having to take care of all the other children.

Mama never understood how I hated life at home during my growing-up years, and she couldn't seem to think of much else but reliving those days. She would get on a one-track idea, and I didn't know what to do to get her off of it. I got so angry, but I never could scream, "Shut up!" I just couldn't talk to her that way even though I wanted to.

By the fall of 1974, I had no money and was running out of medication.

Coping was hard enough with my medication. It was unbearable to imagine going without. I had to have the monies for my doctors and my prescriptions. Nothing else seemed to matter. Bills were piling up, and I was getting desperate. I felt a terrible sense of panic. I had to have my tranquilizers, my mood elevators, and my pain killers. I *needed* my medicine.

On top of all that, Kim had gotten engaged to a nice boy named Dennis Norton, and they planned a November wedding. As mother of the bride, it took a lot of monies to cover the expenses. Where could I get enough monies?

Panicked and desperate, I went to a loan company in Lumberton and put up Mama's house for collateral. I told them that she was too sick to come down in person, and so they gave me the papers to fill out. I forged my mother's name and brought the papers back the next day. I wasn't asked for any kind of identification, and I got the money—a thousand dollars.

Getting the first loan worked all right. Maybe that's why I didn't think too much about it when I took out a second loan for another thousand dollars.

If I had been in my right mind, I would have known that one day I would have to face the repayment of the loan. When I did think about it, and that wasn't often, I told myself that I'd get another job, pay the money back, and Mama would never even know about it.

But I really wasn't thinking about the future. What would happen later wasn't real. The present need for drugs was my only reality. Drugs controlled my life. I could only think of how terrible it would be if I ran out and couldn't get more.

Mama found out—or should have. In early December an overdue notice came addressed to Lillie Bullard from the loan company. Usually I tried to get the mail first, but she got it that time.

"Look at this, will you?" she said. "I wonder why they sent the notice to me? I never took out no loan."

She didn't seem upset, and she threw the notice away. *She knows I did it. She knows. She's going to wait so she can tell everybody what I've done.*

I felt trapped and confused. *What should I do? What can I do? I can't keep putting this off. I have to get a job. I have to replace the monies before Mama finds out. She's going to find out if I don't get a job and replace it.*

Every time the phone rang or anyone came to the house, a wave of fear washed over me. Each day I expected a letter saying that they knew I had forged Mama's name. *I've got to get a job. I've got to get a job to replace the monies.* I was paralyzed by panic. I couldn't do anything. I was trapped, and I had to find a way out. I had to get free from the suffocating guilt.

All different kinds of feelings struggled inside of me—panic and anger and worry about not having any more medication. *What will I do when Mama finds out about the two loans?*

A week after she received the notice about the overdue payment, I went to a nearby town, St. Paul, to pick up medication for myself.

When I went to town to pick up my prescription, I walked around and looked at things.

I saw a bottle of poison, just like what I had bought before. I don't remember thinking about what I would do next. But somewhere inside me, I must have already conceived of the plan. I had done it once, even though I had blotted that from my conscious memory.

I bought the poison and took it home with me.

What am I doing? Oh, no! It's okay. I just want to make her sick for a little while, like Jennings. Except his lungs gave out on him. Then I can get a job and put all the monies back. I knew Mama would be talking to other members of the family, and I didn't want her asking each one of us who signed her name. And, if she went to the loan company, of course, it would be easy to figure out that I was the one just by my handwriting. *You understand, Mama. It's the only way. Just being sick doesn't hurt much.*

About an hour later, Mama started to vomit and complain of diarrhea. She said she had a terrible cramping in her stomach. She hurt bad. But I was so far out of being normal, I couldn't seem to think about her suffering.

I phoned the doctor, "Mama's very sick and needs to see you. Right away."

"How bad sick is she?"

I told him about the vomiting, the cramping, and the diarrhea.

"I'm having a lot of patients with that right now, you know. I can't see everyone who's having the same symptoms." He paused a few seconds. "Tell you what, I'll call the drugstore for something for her. I think it'll make her feel better."

I called a niece, and she drove over to the drugstore to pick up the medicine for Mama. While waiting, I kept thinking of what the doctor had said. *The poison hasn't done this to her. It's something that's going around, like the doctor said. A lot of people are going through the same thing, not just Mama.*

That's how I worked it out in my head.

When my niece returned and I gave Mama the medication, Mama actually got worse. By dark she had gotten so weak that she couldn't sit up anymore.

I called my brother Olive. "Better get the rescue unit and let's take Mama over to the hospital." I explained about calling the doctor earlier. *I'm trying. Nobody can say I'm not trying. I'm getting help for Mama.* While Olive called the rescue unit, I phoned her doctor for the second time and told him what we were doing. The rescue unit, located right around the corner, sent an ambulance immediately to take Mama to the hospital. I rode in the ambulance with her and Olive followed us in his car.

Her doctor arrived shortly after she got there. He stopped and talked to Mama, asking her a lot of questions. "How long have you been sick like this? Where does it hurt now?"

As I listened, I felt panicky, and guilt flooded over me. No matter how I tried to lie to myself, I knew that I had given her poison and that kept troubling me. I was so certain the doctor was going to say, "Someone has poisoned you." I was angry at myself for doing such a thing. *How can a woman do that to her mother?* I didn't have an answer.

The doctor turned to Olive and me. "I'm going to put her in the intensive care unit."

She'll get better. They'll fix whatever is bothering her, and she'll get well soon. I wanted to believe that.

I wanted to confess right then but couldn't. As soon as they examined Mama, I felt positive that they would know what I had done.

Within minutes after they put Mama in intensive care, the doctor came out to us in the waiting area. "I'm sorry, but your mother expired a few minutes ago. She had a massive heart attack."

I broke down, and so did Olive. The doctor tried to comfort us by saying, "She had a long and good life. She's not been well for years, and she didn't suffer much."

I'm not even sure how I got home. Probably Olive drove me. But as soon as I got into the house, I went into the bathroom and fully intended to take every bit of medication I had to end my life. To this day, I don't know why I didn't do that. I hated myself and didn't want to live.

"Mama died because of her heart trouble," I kept repeating aloud. "It had nothing to do with the poison."

"Massive heart attack" the doctor had said. *That's what killed Mama—her heart condition.* I kept telling myself that lie as I gulped down Valium.

The doctor had asked if he could do an autopsy, and I agreed. *Well, they'll find out that way. Then they'll know. I won't say anything, but they'll find out. They always do.*

We didn't get the autopsy back for months. Eventually I received a copy with a long list of things wrong, but they hadn't discovered any poison in her system. *So, the poison had not had any effect on her.* In my sickness I could not admit to myself that something always brings on a massive heart attack. I *wanted* to believe the autopsy.

I never heard another word about the loans. Mama had insurance, and my younger brother Tyrone took care of settling everything. That included paying off anything she owed. I'm sure that he and the others learned about my two forgeries, but they never said a word to me—at least not that I can recall.

I once heard that when people start down a bad road, they don't stop until they reach the bottom. If that's true, I still had a long, long way to go. But I didn't know that then. I didn't think I could sink any lower.

9.

JAILED FOR FRAUD

I moved in with Kim and Dennis who lived in a mobile home. They treated me well, and I enjoyed being with them.

But I had no energy to go out and look for a job. No job meant no money. No money meant that I had no way to buy my medication. I had despised Thomas's weakness for alcohol. Drinking had been his downfall. Yet my addiction to medicines was dragging me to destruction.

I felt more condemned than ever. *If I was any kind of a decent person, I wouldn't have to depend on my prescriptions all the time.*

My kids tried to help me and had been trying for a long time. They had no idea of the shame and humiliation I felt in their trying to help.

Ronnie and Kim sat me down and talked to me as if they were the parents. They told me how I stumbled and fell all over the place, how I was ruining my life. They genuinely worried about me, but it did no good.

"Mama, don't keep doing this to yourself," Kim pleaded as her eyes filled with tears.

Ronnie, just as intense, but not showing so much, said, "Mama, we've talked to doctors. They've told us what happens to people addicted to drugs—any kind of drugs. And you're addicted."

They reasoned and argued with me, and finally they demanded that I do something. I checked in to a mental health center and stayed about two weeks. I didn't tell them that I had been getting prescriptions from several doctors, and they didn't discover how seriously I was addicted. When they released me, they gave me Sinequan, a powerful antidepressant. I added that to my current daily dosages.

I came out in worse condition than before I went to the center. The kids said that I argued more. When they tried to lecture me, I shut them up. "I am taking these medications because doctors have told me to take them. Doctors are smart, and they know more about taking care of people than you do!"

In desperation, the kids stopped arguing with me and decided on a new tactic—separating me from my medication. I wised up to that one quickly and found all kinds of places to hide my medications. I hid pills in my bra, inside pillowcases, wrapped tightly inside clothes in my dresser drawer, inside kitchen cabinets in food containers. They began to search me and my room. One time when I was wearing a hairnet, I put pills there and thought Kim wouldn't find them, but somehow she did.

When they found me passed out from overdoses, they tried to round up all the medication they could find in the room. They knew that as soon as I revived and started moving around, I would take more. They probably stopped me from killing myself through heavy overdoses.

Many times they flushed my medication down the toilet. As I watched, I thought, *Don't they realize how much those pills cost?* Nothing else in the world mattered as much as getting my medication.

When I still lived with my mother, I had discovered an old checkbook of mine. The account had been closed when I married Jennings, but the unused checks hadn't been discarded. When I realized that I had no money to get medication, I remembered the checkbook I had tucked away.

I tried to reason with myself, that if I wrote checks on a closed-out account, I'd never get away with it. But what lay ahead wasn't nearly so real to me as my immediate need for medication.

I went to a drugstore and wrote a check for a medication refill. I told myself that this would help put me right so that I could go out and get another job.

All together I wrote five checks, none of them large, purposely keeping the amounts below forty dollars. I used them at drugstores where I wasn't known so well. Twice I went to the grocery store and bought a few things and got cash. I used that cash for my medication.

Two deputies from the sheriff's department came out to talk to me. They urged me to repay the monies immediately.

"We sent you a letter of warning that unless you repay everything we will have to prosecute you. You did get the letter, didn't you?"

Vaguely I recalled the letter, so I said, "Yes."

But the impact of the warning went past me like everything else. I could not think of consequences. I could live only for the moment.

I had started writing the checks in December, shortly before my mother died, but I wrote at least three of them after I moved in with Kim and Dennis.

"If you don't repay," one deputy said, "the companies will press charges. If they press charges, you'll probably go to jail."

After they left, I thought about going to jail, about my life, and about the things I had done. I despised myself. Suddenly I decided that I really didn't want to live anymore. I decided to die at Ronnie's house.

Ronnie had finished his military service in the Army, and had gotten married. He and his wife also lived in a trailer. One Saturday about lunchtime, I knew they wouldn't be home. He and his wife had gone to play golf. I went to their place, taking with me a combination of sleeping pills, tranquilizers, and pain killers. I don't remember anything after taking the pills.

When they came home, they found me on the floor where I had passed out. They called the rescue unit and took me to the hospital. Apparently when I had passed out from the pills and fallen to the floor, I had broken my collarbone.

I woke up the next morning in the hospital but didn't remember much of anything that had happened. After x-rays had been taken and emergency treatment given, I was taken to the psychiatric unit. I stayed there almost three weeks.

Two men from the sheriff's department came to the hospital to see me. "Mrs. Barfield," one of them said, "we're sorry to have to visit you here like this."

I knew why they had come, of course.

"We have a warrant for your arrest. We can't arrest you while you're in the hospital, but as soon as you get out—"

I nodded, letting them know that I had understood. I may even have promised to repay the monies; I can't remember.

When the hospital released me, I went back to Kim's because I had no place else to go. She and Dennis took me in, but I hated to go there. I already felt so guilty about everything I had done.

I stayed at Kim's two days. On the evening of the second day, a man from the sheriff's department came by. He talked politely but said clearly, so that even I understood, "If you don't pay back the money immediately, you will have to go to court."

Either Kim and Dennis and Ronnie didn't have the money, or else they decided I had to face up to the consequences of what I had done. I only know that two men came the next day and arrested me. They put me in jail until the time of the court hearing.

They hadn't searched me before jailing me. Nobody knew I had brought along a good supply of my pills. The shame of being arrested and put in jail preyed on my mind. Realizing how I had disgraced myself and my family was just too much for me. I overdosed again, taking almost everything I had with me. Someone found me and rushed me to the hospital where my stomach was pumped.

My cell was searched, and the rest of the medication was discovered. Every bit of it was taken away.

The day after I was returned to the jail, I was taken to

court. I pleaded guilty and received a sentence of six months. I was sent to the Correctional Center for Women in Raleigh.

A war was going on inside me all the time. When I had clear days and could think, I realized all the terrible things I had done. But knowing what I had done didn't help. If anything, remembering only made me feel worse.

One evening as I lay in my cell, I asked myself, *What else can happen to me? I can't even successfully do away with myself. I have to be the worst person in the world. No one could sink as low as I have.*

While in the Correctional Center, I went to the mental health unit and told the doctor there about my need for medication. When he saw that I was starting to have withdrawal symptoms, he prescribed Valium. Later he took me off Valium and put me on Elavil. What I didn't understand then, and couldn't explain even to myself, was that guilt had become my worst problem. I tried not to think about that.

I didn't get into any trouble during my four months in prison, even heavily medicated, but I still had a difficult time. We had eighty women in our building. Most of them spent a lot of time in the dayroom, sitting and talking with each other or watching television. I avoided the dayroom and tried to stay by myself because I got too nervous being around the other prisoners. Never any privacy. Even when I decided to walk back to my cell, other inmates would walk by, yelling or talking to me or to each other. My old problem surfaced with even more intensity. Sometimes I felt I would smother unless I could get away from all of them.

Once I walked over to the chapel to get a little quiet and privacy. That didn't work either. People constantly seemed to come and go there as well.

Instead of using those months to think about getting well and to clear my system of drugs, I fantasized about what I'd do when I got out. I kept thinking, even though I wouldn't have admitted it to anyone, that if I could just survive until my release, I knew exactly where I would go. I would hurry to a drugstore and have a prescription filled. I saw myself going through the motions of having the medication handed to me and of my taking it.

Best of all, I wouldn't have to obtain a prescription when I got out. Shortly before my arrest, one doctor had written me a prescription with six refills. I had used only one. All I needed was to remember the approximate date so that I could go to the pharmacist and have him refill it.

No matter how hard I tried to concentrate on other things, my mind constantly returned to that moment of having the druggist hand me a refill. I also planned which doctors I would go to for additional medication.

Because I behaved, I only had to serve four months of the six. I had hardly gotten home before I called the drugstore. They told me I could come in and pick up the refill. Of course I had no money. I took a blank check from my son-in-law's checkbook and forged his name. That paid for my first medication after my prison term.

Again, I didn't consider that Dennis would find out. I thought in terms of *now*, not what will come later. When such thoughts occurred to me, I convinced myself that I could handle it. *I'll get a job right away, just as soon as I can get enough medication to help me function.* I believed my own lies because I wanted to believe them.

How can I explain what it felt like to hold that bottle of pills when the druggist handed it to me? I had waited four months for that moment. I overdosed, not enough to pass out, but enough to blot my actions from my mind.

The worst day for me while I stayed with Kim and Dennis was so bad I still remember nothing about it—only what Kim has since told me. On that day, I had taken so much medication that my mind was a total fog. I didn't pass out, but I felt groggy and lay down on the bed. I fell asleep immediately. That day my parole officer came to the trailer to see me.

Kim woke me, and someone decided that if I took a shower, it would clear my head. But I couldn't even get myself out of bed to do that much. Kim and the parole officer worked together to get me into the shower. But even the shower didn't revive me enough to keep me awake.

"She's going to have to go to a drug treatment center," the officer said.

Kim hated to hear those words. At the same time, though, she knew I needed help. The two of them discussed sending me to a halfway house in Charlotte, North Carolina, so that I could get dried out and off drugs.

The next day my head had cleared enough so that when Kim told me what had happened, I fell apart. I thought of those four months in prison. "No matter what, I can't go back to anything like that."

"Mama, you need help."

"Please, Kim, please, don't let them commit me." I pleaded and wept. I said everything to change her mind. I made wild promises to reform—anything to prevent being sent away again.

Both Kim and Dennis tried to explain about the drug treatment center and how I needed help. "It's what you need. And it won't be a long time—"

They pleaded, trying to make me want to go on my own. I was determined I would never go there. I did my best that day and—at the time—I also meant my words. "Please, don't send me. I know I've got a problem with medications. I'll kick it. I promise. Just give me a chance to prove to you that I can do it by myself. Please don't send me there."

"I don't want to send you," Kim said, the tears streaming down her cheeks, "but you've got to have help, Mama. You can't go on like this."

"I know that now. I really know it. I'll stop taking these medications. I promise!"

How long did that scene go on? For hours? Probably not, but it seemed that way. In the end, Dennis called the parole officer. "We're working with her. She's determined to break the habit and we're going to work with her."

Reluctantly the parole officer agreed not to push for my

commitment. She made them promise that if I got bad again, they would tell her.

I made an effort to show my family that I meant it. I never stopped taking drugs, but I cut down the amount, taking barely enough so that I felt the effects but not so much that anyone could detect it. When I cut down, my system begged for additional medication. I kept lying to myself, saying that I was working my way off medication. In reality, I was only trying to figure out a way to get away from Kim and Dennis so that I could have my medications without their knowing it.

It didn't take long before I found a way. I simply moved out. "Kim, honey, you're pregnant. You don't need the extra problem of having me in this cramped place," I told her.

She was expecting her first child. She also believed I was better and that I had started cutting myself off medications.

"Mama, if you're not here, I'll worry about you."

I worked around that, too. I found a kind of job—one with no heavy demands on me. I started living with an older lady. I watched out for her during the day, and in exchange I had my own room and my privacy after she went to bed.

The woman had some kind of mental problem, and her sister didn't want her staying alone. She did strange things like turning on the stove and letting everything in the pan burn. Or she would turn on the water and leave it running. Her sister hired me to watch out for her and see that she caused herself no harm.

I functioned during that time, but my job didn't demand much either.

The woman kept getting worse and demanding more and more attention. After I had stayed with her for four months, her sister finally put her in a mental institution.

I soon got another position, but in the meantime my drug consumption went back to where it had been before.

Kim and Dennis realized what had happened, and they didn't know what to do. They tried to help the way many family members do. They searched for my pills. When they found them, they flushed them down the toilet or took them out of the house and threw them away. I had been through that before, but I couldn't say too much. I was so afraid that they would call the parole officer and that I'd have to go to the drug treatment center. Two or three times Kim found the doctor's name on a bottle and called him. "Please don't prescribe any more medicine for my mother."

As soon as she made a call like that, I knew I would just have to spend additional money to visit a new doctor to start the prescriptions going.

The four months in prison had done me no good. I was back where I had started.

10.

FLASHBACKS

A new position opened up immediately. An elderly woman, Dollie Edwards, visited her invalid husband in the hospital. She wanted to bring him home but couldn't take care of him by herself. The doctor had told her, "The only way it will work is if you get help at home. Someone to live in and take care of Mr. Edwards."

Dollie got acquainted with a county nurse, the woman who had hired me to take care of her sister. They talked about Dollie's situation and the nurse told her about me. The next day Dollie called. After a few minutes' conversation, she hired me.

Dollie furnished me with room and board and seventy-five dollars a week. The Edwardses lived only a mile from Kim and Dennis, and it relieved Kim to know that she was close by if I needed her.

The seventy-five dollars took care of my medication, but it wasn't enough when I had to see the doctor and pay for an office visit.

I went to work for the Edwardses around the first of November 1975. Her husband, Montgomery, nine or ten years older than Dollie, was ninety-three. He was a tiny fellow who probably didn't weigh one hundred pounds. Not only was he a complete invalid, he was blind. Dollie, taller and heavier, probably weighed 155 pounds. They were fairly well off. Besides their home, they owned some other property.

Dollie did most of the cooking, and I took care of Mr. Edwards. Each day I bathed and fed him and did anything else he wanted. Sometimes he slept for long periods of time, and I would have to wake him up to give him the little bit of medication he needed.

I didn't like being there and felt depressed most of the time. *I need to get out of here.* But my numbed mind could not figure out how to go about leaving. Or maybe I was so badly confused that I didn't have the ability to follow through on my own intentions.

After I had been with the Edwardses for nearly a year, I met Dollie's nephew, Stuart Taylor, at the Edwardses' home in Lumberton. It was September 1976.

Stuart owned a tobacco farm and had been married three times. His first wife had died, the second marriage had ended in divorce. He and his third wife had separated, and they were talking divorce when we met. Dollie had told me all about him.

She called him an alcoholic, but said, "He's different from most kinds because he doesn't drink every day. He'll go for weeks at a time without touching a drop. Then he goes on a real binge that sometimes lasts two or three weeks."

I liked Stuart when I first met him. He was fair complexioned, balding with gray hair, about five feet nine, heavyset but not fat. He wore glasses and was ten years my senior.

After Dollie had introduced us, the three of us sat around and talked for maybe an hour. Stuart included me in the conversation, and I appreciated his thoughtfulness.

A few days later Stuart came back. As he was getting ready to leave, he turned to me and said, "Velma, how about going out to eat with me tomorrow night?"

"I'd like to do that." *It will be wonderful to get away from the house.*

I enjoyed the time together. Stuart had a way of making me laugh, and he paid attention when I talked, even about little things. In his presence, I didn't feel quite so depressed or alone.

It got to be a regular habit for him to come by for me. We'd go out to eat, usually at a seafood or barbecue place. We did this for a month, maybe six weeks. Then he stopped coming without any explanation.

I mentioned to Mrs. Edwards, "Stuart hasn't been around lately."

"Oh, he and his wife have started talking about getting together again."

"I hope it does work out for them," I said. Although I missed Stuart, I really hoped they would get back together.

After that single conversation, Mrs. Edwards never mentioned him. I assumed that he and his wife had straightened everything out.

In the meantime, I continued to work at the Edwardses' home, and the tension started building up inside me again. I found myself hating to get up in the mornings. I went to bed earlier and earlier each night. Sleep and medication seemed to be the only things that gave me any kind of peace.

When I bathed Mr. Edwards, Dollie watched everything I did. She talked the whole time, too. "Now, don't use too much of that baby oil. You don't need that much."

When I put talcum powder on him, she said, "That's way too much, Velma. I want you to use less next time. We can't just keep wasting all of that powder."

That irritated me, and it kept building up because I couldn't say anything to her. The situation got worse. In his condition, Mr. Edwards couldn't control his urine or his bowels, and he frequently messed up his bed. I wanted to clean him up and to put on clean linens each time. She complained about using so many sheets.

"Just spread rubber sheeting over the mattress."

I couldn't stand the thought of doing that. Rubber sheeting left such a foul odor. The resentment built up because she did not like my changing the sheets and told me to stop.

Changing sheets each time meant having to run the washing machine two or three times a week. I don't think she was a stingy woman, but she had it fixed in her mind about using the washing machine. "We only need to use that once a week. Once. That's all."

At times I felt that I saw flashbacks, as if I had gone back home again. She acted like my mother—always telling me what to do and never pleased with the way I did things. At times when she spoke I could hear my mother saying, "Go on and do it like I told you to."

Over the last few months, the pressure had built up so much that every time Mrs. Edwards started to complain, I wanted to scream at her. I never did, but I wanted to. I began to hate Mrs. Edwards. I wanted to hurt her in some way.

Mr. Edwards died around the first of the year, 1977, but I stayed on to live with Dollie. In March I went shopping. While I was downtown, I saw the same kind of poison that I had bought before. I bought a bottle and took it home with me.

That evening, I poisoned her. The next day she went through a terrible period of pain, but I had so medicated myself that I felt divorced from her suffering. *Why is she writhing and groaning?* I made no connection between giving her the poison and seeing her reaction. *She is elderly and must not be well.*

Dollie Edwards died the next day.

11.

THE NEXT TWO VICTIMS

A few days after Dollie died, I received a telephone call. "Would you consider staying with my parents?" The woman explained, "Mom broke her leg, and she's getting up there in years. My dad can't wait on her the way she needs." She agreed to pay me fifty dollars a week, twenty-five dollars less than the Edwardses paid me.

I agreed to move in with her parents, beginning the first part of April 1977.

John Henry Lee was eighty, short, perhaps five-feet-six, almost bald, and weighed a hundred and sixty pounds. Record, his wife, was an inch or two shorter, heavyset, and gray haired.

Mrs. Lee talked a lot, and before I had been there a month I knew most of their life story. They had had a rocky marriage through all their years together. He had been unfaithful to her early in their marriage, and she had never gotten over it.

"I still don't trust him. When he says he's going to a certain place, I can never believe him."

They argued a lot, constantly bickering over things of no importance. She often got upset and went into her room, refusing to sit in the living room with him.

Sometimes I wanted to shout, "Why don't both of you shut up!"

Having to listen to their bickering increased the pressure,

and I kept wanting to find some way to get out of that place. *I can't stand much more of this.*

I needed the income, small as it was, to keep me in my medications. I couldn't just walk out, and yet I couldn't stay either. I began to feel resentful and angry. *If I don't get out of this place, I'll explode.*

I decided that the only way to get out of that place would be to poison Mr. Lee. *He hired me, and he is the one who pays me. She is not important.*

I don't know how long I would have continued that way, but something happened that forced me to take some kind of action. I had to see a new doctor. That meant monies for the office visit as well as for the medication itself. I took one of Mr. Lee's blank checks, made it payable to some woman's name I made up, and signed the check as John Henry Lee. I made it payable for fifty dollars.

When the bank statement came, I knew he would have to know that I had done it. In a state of panic, I again bought poison, telling myself that I only wanted to make him sick so that I could leave, get a different job, and replace the monies I had taken by forgery.

I know that doesn't make sense, but to my tired, medicated brain, filled with twenty pills a day, it made perfect sense.

In the late summer of 1977, I poisoned him. He went through the same kinds of pain that the others had gone through. Again, I watched in a detached way, feeling no connection between my actions and his pain.

When he died, the medical report said he had died of a heart attack. Mr. Lee did have a bad heart.

See, that poison didn't kill him. It only made him sick. His heart condition finally killed him.

"What a surprise!" I said as I opened the door for Stuart Taylor to come in. "I haven't seen you in a year, I guess."

"Has been quite a while," he said as he came into the living room.

We talked, as friendly as ever, but he said nothing about

his absence or his wife. A few days later he finally said that they were in the process of divorce but that it would not be final until May of 1978.

After showing up that day, Stuart got into the habit of riding over to Mrs. Lee's every day to see me. Often we went out to eat in the evening.

The family of Mr. Lee wanted me to stay with Record, and so I remained there for two more months. After Mr. Lee's death, the pressure did not lessen, and I knew I had to get out of that place. Memories as much as anything haunted me, reminding me of what I had done to Mr. Lee. I didn't want to think about it.

I finally left because I decided not to stay with people anymore. I wanted to live alone and get a regular job again. I moved back to Lumberton and rented a trailer for myself. I got a job in Lumberton at a nursing home where I worked as a nurse's aide. They put me on the third shift, and I went to work at eleven at night.

Stuart and I continued to see each other regularly. He knew I took medication "for my nerves," but he had no idea how much—I carefully kept that from him. A few times he went with me to the drugstore to pick up a prescription. I tried to make my explanation sound as if taking the medication was a temporary thing.

Stuart would come every day for two or three weeks then suddenly disappear for several days. This became his pattern. Sometimes a whole week passed before I would hear from him again. One time I didn't see him for three weeks. I called his stepmother, asking about him.

"He's not well," she said.

"Oh, I hope it's not anything serious—"

We talked a little more before she finally said, "He's been on one of his drinking times again."

After three weeks, Stuart showed up at my trailer with no explanation. He acted as if he had been there only the day before.

If my mind hadn't been so fuzzy, I would have realized that

I didn't want to get into that kind of situation. I should have seen that I had begun to repeat the pattern of life with Thomas.

Stuart gradually became more open with his drinking—sometimes coming to see me while he was intoxicated. Those times we argued. We argued about a lot of things, but mostly about his drinking. At the time I didn't realize it, but I started saying the same things to him that I had said to Thomas. Many of his words sounded like Thomas's.

More than once he left in a half-drunken, angry state. On those occasions, I called out after him, "I wish you'd never come back."

For two or three weeks after an incident like that, he stayed away. Then he would show up at my door, acting as if nothing had happened.

I welcomed him back because I had missed him. Besides, I enjoyed his company. We had many miserable times together, but when he was away, I felt even emptier than before.

Despite his drinking problem, we grew more and more attached to each other. We started to talk about marriage. I don't know if I loved him or not. Sometimes I felt certain I did, especially when he came over sober and we had a quiet time together.

I moved some of my things into his house. I got off work at seven in the morning and went over there two or three times a week, slept there during the day, spent the rest of the time with Stuart, and went back to work in the evening.

Besides clothes, I had several personal items at his house. Among those items were several letters I had received while in prison. I had never told Stuart about my imprisonment.

One morning when I came home from work, Stuart was in the bedroom waiting for me. He held up the letters. "Why didn't you tell me you had been in prison?"

I felt angry that he had gone through my personal things. We started to argue.

Again he said, "Why didn't you tell me you had been in prison?"

"I didn't want anybody to know."

"Not even me?"

"Especially you."

"Especially me? I'm the man you planned to marry."

"I'm ashamed of what I did and of ever having gone to prison. I hoped that you'd never find out."

"Well, I did find out!"

I suddenly realized that he had been drinking.

"Okay, Stuart, now you know. I won't try to hide anything from you again. But, please, don't tell anybody."

"I'm going to tell anybody I want to."

"Please—"

"If anybody asks me anything about you, I won't keep it hid. I want everyone to know that Velma Barfield has been in prison!"

We argued some more, but his cruel words cut deep and twisted inside me. Whatever love I thought I had for him died. I never again felt comfortable around him. I resented Stuart's reaction to my prison record. I felt he wanted to hurt me deeply—and I still think that. Whenever we had arguments after that, he managed to twist things around and bring up the subject of my prison term.

In November 1977, I stole one of his blank checks and forged his name. When he discovered what happened, the angry words flew between us. He threatened to call the police and turn me in.

He scared me because I remembered those four months in prison. "Please, please, don't report me! Please, Stuart, I promise that I'll pay you back. Every penny!"

"Okay," he said after a long argument, "just forget it. You don't need to pay it back."

"But I will—"

"Forget it," he said again.

I never did pay him back because I think he really meant that I didn't have to. Yet whenever we got into arguments, he brought up the forged check again. He kept threatening to turn me in.

I had breast surgery that winter. There was no malignancy, but a portion of my left breast was removed. When I was released from the hospital, I planned to stay with Kim until I could go back to work. Stuart came over to see me, however, and he asked me to stay with him instead.

We had a terrible time together. He treated me badly. Even though I was recovering from surgery, he offered me no sympathy. The arguments went on.

Although I eventually went back to work, I had received no income during the five-week period of my surgery and recuperation. Despite the problems forging one of Stuart's checks had caused me, I forged a second one. I was desperate for monies again. I needed additional medication and had to pay a doctor's fee. As a nurse's aide, I made only minimum wage, and most of my money went for my medicine.

Not long after that I had to go back to the doctor for a post-surgery checkup. He gave me a prescription, and I went to the drugstore to get it filled. As soon as the pharmacist handed me the medication, I bought a Coke and took one of the capsules.

As I sipped my Coke, I began to worry about replacing the monies. It was nearly time for Stuart to get a new bank statement. *But if he's sick, he won't feel like looking over the bank statement. If he's sick, he'll just let it pile up, and in the meantime I can figure out how to replace the money.*

On the way home, I stopped and bought another bottle of poison. I hadn't really thought about it, but that afternoon I knew what I was going to do. The seriousness of it didn't get through to me.

My thinking was so distorted by years of heavy medication that even though I knew what I was doing, I couldn't connect poisoning him with the suffering he would go through. By that time, poison was my antidote to the unbearable. I knew it would help. It had helped before, even if only temporarily. It was all I could figure out to do.

I knew what would happen to him, as it had happened to

the others. Yet I couldn't relate to his pain. I had started on a new pain killer that day, mixed with quantities of Valium and Elavil and perhaps one or two other medications. My thinking was so twisted that my mind was in a stupor. It was as though I saw myself poisoning him, and yet it was as if someone else had done it. I had no control over my actions.

That evening, we went to a Rex Humbard gospel meeting. During all this time I had been going to church, although not as regularly as I had before. Stuart and I had decided to go to the meeting because he liked the music.

During the meeting, Stuart started to get sick. The longer we stayed, the more guilty I felt. *We're in this religious meeting and I poisoned Stuart. God, what have I done? I poisoned him. Oh, my God! What can I do? What have I done?*

After maybe half an hour, he said, "I'm too sick to stay. I've got to get outside." I didn't know what to do. I stayed for the rest of the meeting while he waited in the car.

When we returned to the house and I realized how sick he was, I called his stepmother and his daughter. I told them, "Stuart's very sick."

Stuart could hear me talking. I told them that I had suggested he go to the doctor but that he refused. Even when he started vomiting and the pain showed no sign of letting up, he still refused to go.

"If you get any worse, I'm taking you to see a doctor," I said. *I'm trying to help.*

He did get worse. On the second day after the poisoning, I persuaded him to let me carry him to the emergency room.

The doctor said it sounded like a flu virus that was going around. "Get him home to bed and give him lots of fluids."

He wrote a prescription for Stuart. After taking him home again and putting him into bed, I went out and got it filled. He took the medicine, but, if anything, it made it worse.

Late in the evening of the third day, Stuart still had no relief from his pain. He was so weak. He had eaten nothing for the past three days.

I phoned a neighbor who worked for the highway patrol

and asked him to call the rescue unit to take Stuart to the hospital. He phoned them, and I followed the ambulance in Stuart's truck.

As soon as I arrived at the hospital, I called his family to tell them. Stuart had been at the hospital less than an hour when he died.

I heard the doctor saying something to the family members about additional tests. "I'd like to do an autopsy, too," the doctor said. One of the daughters asked me, "What do you think?"

"I think it's a good idea." I didn't expect them to find anything. Besides, my mind was already convincing me that I had not killed Stuart. *I made him sick, but he had caught the flu. That's what killed him.*

For the next few weeks, I went back to my solitary life, living for the time I got off work so that I could medicate myself. Once at work, I counted the hours until I would be home and could medicate myself again.

On March 10, 1978, the doorbell rang. Even though it was in the afternoon, I was heavily drugged. I had not done anything since getting off work except sleep.

When I finally made my way to the door and opened it, I saw the man who introduced himself as Detective Phillips.

12.

ALONE NO MORE

When I confessed, I wanted to tell everything and get rid of the heavy load that I had carried for such a long time. It came as a relief that at last I could tell someone what I had done.

The relief I experienced was temporary. As soon as I re-medicated myself, the same old guilt, pressures, and confusion took over again. The only good feeling I had was in saying to myself, *Well, at last they know everything.*

I was still filled with anger and hatred. I suspected everyone of being out to get me.

My court-appointed lawyer, Bob Jacobson, received a report from Dorothea Dix stating that I was found competent to stand trial. Mr. Jacobson arranged for me to see another psychiatrist, and a deputy took me to him in Lumberton. I spent no more than thirty minutes with him, and then he also declared me competent to stand trial.

Nobody talked to me about my bitterness and anger, about my pattern of medication, about my past problems with Thomas, or even about my troubled childhood. They didn't ask, and in my confused state, I never volunteered anything.

At the time of my arrest, I was still going to church. I heard the preaching and listened (when I could concentrate), and everybody accepted me as one of them. Once or twice I wondered how they would treat me if they knew what I was really like inside.

I had been attending a Pentecostal church, and the pastor hadn't visited me during the weeks at Dix. He came by the jail one time to see me. He was apologetic when he came.

"I didn't visit you there at Dorothea Dix," he said, "because I was afraid I would upset you emotionally and that would interfere with the evaluation they were doing."

He stayed about three minutes, and he never came again. He didn't know what to do or to say. Another time three or four ladies from that church came to the jail and visited a few minutes with me and the other inmates.

Several other women were in jail, too, but no one shared my cell or was even in a cell close by. I had no one to talk to and felt that no one cared. I sat in the dayroom outside my cell too depressed to do anything. I was so miserable. I reached one of the lowest points during the eight months I stayed in jail.

A jail matron broke my solitude one Thursday. "Velma, my pastor is here. I wanted him to come by and say hello to you."

Hope flickered in me. *Maybe someone will listen and talk to me.*

The matron introduced us as the pastor walked into the dayroom. He looked right at me. Without any other words, he said, "I want you to tell me what in the world caused you to do what you did."

I burst into tears. I thought I had reached the lowest point possible, but after that statement I felt even worse. The pain hurt so deeply inside, I couldn't have talked if I had wanted to.

He turned away from me and walked down to one of the other cells. He started talking to another prisoner. Later I heard him pray for her.

I returned to my cell. More than at any other time, I wanted to kill myself. I had thought of suicide for days and had already determined to do it. I tried to figure out how. I could think of only two possible solutions. I could save my pills until I had enough for an overdose. Or I could figure out how to hang myself with the sheets. I didn't care how I did it, I only wanted to die. I wasn't fit to live with other people.

By Saturday night I had decided on the solution—saving up medication. On that night in July 1978, I lay in my bunk thinking of my misery and guilt. I sobbed. *I want to die. I want to die.*

Usually anywhere from two to five women occupied the other cells—they always kept me in a cell by myself—but on that particular Saturday night, I was the only woman prisoner. Totally alone, I could weep and cry out in my pain. No one was around to hear me and laugh.

The guard had his radio tuned in to a twenty-four hour gospel station in Laurinburg, North Carolina. I had been half listening throughout the evening, but I wasn't really aware of the programs. I was too wrapped up in my own plan of self-destruction.

Then, as it never had before, my guilt hit me. Every terrible thing I had ever done in my life—from childhood on—came to my mind and would not go away. Guilt overwhelmed me. I had actually *killed* people. For the first time, the reality of those murders began to seep through—not clearly and not fully—but enough so that I knew I couldn't ever again face another human being. *Everyone can see the guilt and the hatred in my face. No one can understand me or have compassion for me because I don't deserve any.*

The guard turned out the lights at 9:00, but I didn't go to sleep. I lay in the dark, wanting to die right then. I didn't even want to wait until I had saved up enough medication. I thrashed back and forth. *I'm so miserable and hateful and worthless.*

At 11:00, the first strains of the chorus, "Allelujah," filtered through to my cell. A new program had started, and the music caught my attention. I had heard that simple chorus hundreds of times before, but it had never sounded the same. I sat up, straining to hear every note of the music.

As soon as the song finished, a man's powerful voice came on. "No matter where you are tonight or what's happening to you, somebody loves you!"

Nobody could ever love me. Not after what I've done.

"Yes, somebody loves you and His name is Jesus! He loves you tonight no matter where you are or what you've done. That same Jesus is standing at the door of many hearts tonight, knocking, waiting to come inside, and wanting to put a new spirit within you."

I felt as if God spoke directly to me through that evangelist J. K. Kinkle. No matter what kind of objections I raised in my mind, I would hardly think of them before he would say something to dispute them.

"Won't you open your heart's door and let Jesus come inside? He'll give you a new heart and a new spirit."

I'd heard those words all my life and could repeat them as well as anybody. But this time they sounded different. I understood that I had never allowed Jesus Christ to really enter into my life and let Him live with me. Despite all the teachings I had received over the years, that idea had never penetrated until that moment.

I couldn't stop the tears. I felt as if my insides were being ripped apart from the pain. For two hours I had been lying on my bunk in darkness, crushed and so alone. And yet, for the first time, I sensed a ray of hope. *But not for me. Not after all I've done—*

"Yes! You can be forgiven. It's so simple. Invite Him in! Confess your sins to Him this minute. Let Him make you a new person and give you a new beginning. Do it! Do it now!"

God loves me. No matter what I have done, He is ready to forgive me.

I had been in and out of churches all my life and I could explain all about God. But I had never understood before that Jesus had died for *me.* That comforting thought would not leave me as the tears continued to flow.

The horror of my life, ever since childhood, had been unbearable. How could I ever hope to be clean? Suddenly, all that I had ever heard or known about Christianity hit home. I couldn't be free on my own. I couldn't ever find forgiveness on my own. But the marvelous revelation was that God knew that. He knew that I was hopeless without Him. And that's why He sent His only son. Jesus, who was blameless, paid the penalty *for* me because I couldn't. It was as simple as that! All my life I was weighted down by my sins because I couldn't do better. It never occurred to me that Jesus really did pay the price, that Jesus alone bore the extreme punishment— death—for *my* sins, not just for my "good" neighbors. And, even more glorious, Jesus is willing to be my friend even now. I can talk to Him, and He will listen.

All the past years swam before my eyes. If only I had known that I could talk to Jesus and that He truly cared and listened. When I was a child, if only I had known that I could have prayed whenever I felt so alone and that nobody cared. My guilt had been such a heavy burden. If only I could have said many years ago, "Jesus, please help me." I couldn't undo my grievous sins. I couldn't bring those people back to life. It was too late to go back. It's always too late to go back. But I realized at that time that I could go *forward*.

I kept hearing the words of that evangelist telling me, "Jesus loves you." Timidly at first, I started to confess my sins—everything I had done wrong that came to mind, including the killing of those people. As I whispered aloud between my sobs, it became easier.

All that deep-seated hatred and bitterness in me didn't leave, but I did feel better. I knew I had been forgiven, and I understood that God loved me. For the first time in my entire forty-three years of life, I had peace.

I didn't understand much about my experience. Drugs still clouded my thinking a lot of the time. But on that Saturday night, I knew that God had gotten through to me and that I would never be the same again. I thought of verses I had memorized and quoted years earlier without understanding. Now I knew what they meant. "Therefore, if any man be in Christ, he is a new creature..." (2 Corinthians 5:17 KJV).

I had a long way to go. But I had received enough of God's peace to know that I would never be alone again.

13.

THE TRIAL

After my dramatic experience with God, my life became different—and yet none of the facts had changed. The D.A. charged me with first-degree murder, and I still faced trial.

My attorney warned me that if I was found guilty, the jury might impose the death sentence. At the same time, however, he reminded me that no woman had been executed in the United States since 1962. It was a matter of "expect the best but prepare for the worst."

I wrote to Kim to prepare her without alarming her. "It might go very bad for me," is about as strong as I could put it. I did tell her also, "Jesus will go into the courtroom with me." That's as much as I could talk about my conversion at that point.

During the trial, Ronnie and Kim gave me a lot of emotional support and even seemed to be aware of how sick I was. My brothers and sisters also rallied behind me. Their support helped, but I had another helper—I now had God in my life in a way I never had before.

I was a new creature, and my first steps didn't come easy. I had ups and downs, and except for a quietness coming from the center of my being, nothing outward had changed. I knew almost nothing about God and prayer, even though I had been in and out of churches most of my life.

Learning to cope better with my situation came slowly. Except for the five weeks I had been at Dorothea Dix, I stayed in the same jail cell in Lumberton until the trial started the last week of November—eight and a half months. My conversion had taken place midway.

Changes—very slow ones—began to take place in my life. For one thing, my attitude toward the guards changed. Previously I had felt only bitterness toward them, convinced they would do anything they could against me. I learned to see them as people who had a job to do.

In the middle of the summer, some of us prisoners badly wanted a drink of cold water. When we turned on the faucet, the water came out hot. We asked a matron if she would bring us cold water, and she refused. As I began to grow in my newly found faith, I began to understand people like the matron. I didn't like the things they did (or refused to do), but I no longer built up resentment against them.

It was hard for me to learn to accept even small failings in others. My whole life had been a defense against people who I thought were trying to make my life miserable. But the awareness of God's mercy that I first experienced that July night was becoming clearer.

Who was I to bear grudges over such trivial irritations when God has forgiven *my* enormous sins? I wondered, *If I were God, would I have forgiven me?* I didn't know the answer to that. But God's mercy had broken through the ugliness of my misspent life to reach the Velma Barfield that could have been all along, the Velma Barfield created in the image of God.

It is easy to follow Christ with words, harder with actions, harder yet with attitude.

No one encouraged me, probably because I didn't talk about my conversion much. Even though I had all those years of going to church, I didn't know how to explain about what had happened to me. I tried to tell one person, and she said, "But I thought you already were a Christian."

It wasn't easy to talk about, and I didn't want people to

think I had turned to God just to get out of a severe sentence. I knew that something had happened to me.

I owned a Bible, and I had Ronnie bring it to me in jail. Every day I read from it. I couldn't believe the difference. Words and passages that I had heard or read before suddenly were filled with new meaning—and it seemed like God was saying it just for me. I was amazed at how every little piece fit together with my life, sort of like a jigsaw puzzle when the first few pieces go together and you know you're going to be able to put the whole thing together if you just keep at it long enough. Yet I had no idea of how to study the Bible. My study consisted mostly of reading random chapters and frequent rereading of the Psalms.

I also prayed. In my immature and confused way, most of my prayers consisted of telling God about my children and my needs and asking for His help. It was a beginning. And what a comforting beginning. I talked and talked to God. And he listened; I knew He listened. I found that whenever I was troubled about anything, I could tell God about it. For someone like me, who had gone through life shadow-boxing her troubles, ignorant of the true enemy, it was a welcome relief. I talked, God listened. It would be a while before I knew it worked the other way, too—God would talk, I would listen.

At the same time I continued with my medication as much as before. It hadn't occurred to me yet to get rid of my addiction.

I wrote to J. K. Kinkle, the radio evangelist whose message had brought me to Jesus Christ. I told him what had happened to me during his broadcast. Someone who helped with his prison work replied to my letter and rejoiced with me in my new faith. She enclosed literature for me to read.

About that same time, one of the other prisoners loaned me her copy of George Beverly Shea's autobiography. The story of that great singer's simple commitment was inspiring. I wrote to the Billy Graham Association and told them that I had become a Christian only a short time earlier. I asked them to send me any literature they could.

Within days I had a kind letter from them, and a few days after, a package of books. The one I liked best, *Norma*, told the life story of singer Norma Zimmer. *Joni*, about quadriplegic Joni Eareckson Tada, made me realize how available God is to us when we turn our lives over to Him. I also enjoyed the story of country singer Johnny Cash, *The Man in Black*.

I lay on my bunk and read as fast as I could, which wasn't very fast in those days. Medication kept my mind dulled so much of the time that I found it difficult to read rapidly. At times it was impossible to comprehend what I had read, but I kept on anyway.

After my trial and subsequent conviction, I took those books to prison with me where I finished them during my first weeks of adjustment. It helped to have the books with me during the dark and lonely hours.

I remember so little about the trial itself. Originally the trial should have been held at the county seat in Lumberton, but it was changed first to Laurinburg and then to Elizabethtown. The state of North Carolina had charged me only with Stuart's death. I never confessed to poisoning Jennings Barfield, even though traces of poison were found in his body after he was exhumed. I can give no reason for not confessing except that I was in a crazy, confused state of mind during those years. But because I had voluntarily confessed to poisoning my mother, Dollie Edwards, and John Henry Lee, the district attorney made frequent references to their deaths, charging me with following a pattern of cold-blooded calculation.

They tell me that I argued with the D.A., Mr. Joe Freeman Britt. Even though I had confessed to the other killings, when he mentioned my poisoning the others, I interrupted. "But the medical report says my mother died of a heart attack, that Mr. Lee—" Deep within I knew differently, yet I couldn't help myself. I had convinced myself so thoroughly that they died of other causes that I didn't want to believe otherwise.

Mr. Britt angered me. One time I found myself thinking, *I'd like to hit him or something.* The spiritual change I had experienced was opposed by years of defensive reactions. I was still wearing my old habits like outgrown clothes. They didn't fit anymore, but I clung to the familiar, not sure how to let go. I was still angry at almost everybody. I vaguely recall being on the stand and arguing with him. My attorney later told me that my arguments with the D.A. had a great deal of negative influence with the jury.

My son, Ronald Burke, remembers what happened:

Mr. Jacobson asked Mama to cooperate with him. He tried to coach her on how to behave in the courtroom so that she could draw sympathy from the jury. He spent a lot of time patiently explaining this to her.

He questioned whether to put her on the stand. He and I talked about it, and finally he decided to let her testify. One of the last things he said to her was, "If you feel like crying, go ahead and cry."

That's not how Mama acted when she got on the stand. She argued with the district attorney when he said she intended to kill the victims.

Mama insisted that the authorities had performed autopsies in each case and that they hadn't found any poison. She kept saying that she never intended to kill anyone, even though she admitted [poisoning them]. But she kept saying, "I only meant to make them sick."

During the trial I think she had some hope that she was going to be found not guilty. She didn't think about the sentence. I don't think any of us did.

From the defense side, there wasn't a lot to the trial. Mr. Jacobson called in two psychiatrists, only one of whom actually came to court. Both testified that she was capable of standing trial. One of them was a doctor who had been prescribing medicine for her when she was brought in for questioning. The court accepted a written deposition from the doctor because he was sick and in the hospital.

The other psychiatrist was a resident at [a mental health center], but I don't think he really knew much about Mama. The court was trying to find out if she was sane and competent to stand trial. That's what I think the problem was. The fact is, she was sane, but she wasn't competent to stand trial. She couldn't help her own case, and she ended up making it worse by not cooperating.

Dee Reid of the *North Carolina Independent*, a bi-weekly newspaper printed in Durham, North Carolina, would later profile the district attorney, Joe Freeman Britt, in an article, "The Case of the Deadly DA," July 20–August 2, 1984:

> "...What I try to do is make the jury identify with the victim," he once told *The News and Observer*.. "If you can make that victim get up and walk right out of the grave, then you can make the jury see him."
>
> Britt did the next best thing during the trial of Velma Barfield.... Britt asked an ambulance attendant to demonstrate to the court the pain the victim experienced in his last moments. According to the trial transcript, the witness complied, throwing back his head and letting out a bloodcurdling scream.

About 6:30 P.M. on Saturday, the jury reconvened, and I was brought back in to court. The jury had been out less than three hours.

Judge McKinnon presided. He asked the foreman if the jury had reached a verdict.

"Yes, we have, your honor."

"How do you find the defendant?"

"Guilty of murder in the first degree."

I heard the foreman tell the judge, "We recommend the death penalty."

Kim and Ronnie had been sitting next to me at the table. I looked over at Kim, and even though she made no noise, she cried uncontrollably. For me, the shock impact took away the sting of the sentence. I didn't think of what the words meant, I could only watch my daughter sobbing. "God, have mercy," I whispered. I felt choked up, and although I wanted to cry, I held it back. I couldn't say anything to Kim because I had no words of comfort for her. To say anything might make it worse. I didn't know how much more she could handle. I prayed silently, *Lord, help me not to fall apart. Help me keep myself together for Kim's sake.*

Kim's husband, Dennis, led her out of the courtroom. I

watched helplessly as she left. Her heart-wrenching sobs nearly tore me apart.

As the bailiff led me away, my chest felt crushed, as if I couldn't breathe. I had been given extra medication during the week of the trial, and each day after taking what I needed, I kept some back. I had planned to use it at the end of the trial to take my life. It hadn't occurred to me that killing myself was as much a sin as killing anyone else. I was looking for a way out, for my kids as much as for me. Or so I thought. *How can they live with the disgrace of a convicted murderer for a mother? How can I live with myself? Why should God want me to live? What use is my life to anybody?* When I got back to my cell, I took three of the antidepressant tablets I had hidden away. But I had no plans then to kill myself. At that moment, I simply didn't want to think or to feel anything. I just wanted to make it through the night the only way I knew. I hadn't yet learned to turn to God for strength. The pills put me to sleep for the entire night.

On Sunday morning, Ronnie brought his son to see me. When I saw little Tommy, all my self-control vanished, and I fell apart. The verdict finally penetrated my drugged mind. I would never live to see three-year-old Tommy grow up. I started to weep then and couldn't stop.

I lay in a depressed state the rest of the weekend. On Monday morning, two deputies took me from the Elizabethtown jail and drove me to the Correctional Center for Women in Raleigh, where I had been imprisoned earlier for writing worthless checks. This time it would not be the same. Previously I had been sentenced for only a short time and had stayed in an open unit with free access to the grounds. This time I would be confined to death row. I would not be coming back. Even if the courts later commuted my sentence to life imprisonment, I would stay on death row a long time because of the lengthy appeals process. It would be years before I could know my final destiny.

As we drove out of Elizabethtown, the impact of what I was leaving behind hit me—my kids and grandkids, my brothers and sisters, even the privilege of making choices.

14.

PRISON

The two deputies treated me as nicely as anyone could. I was so broken up, I could hardly sit still as we drove on. Although I tried not to, I cried and couldn't stop myself. The driver pulled off the road, went into a restaurant, and bought me a Coke. They weren't supposed to do that, and I felt so grateful for that kindness.

When we arrived at Raleigh, they went with me past the front gate—which was as far as they really had to take me— and stayed with me all the way to the administration building. I felt as if they wanted to show me special attention that they weren't required to give.

We arrived at the prison at 1:30, and by 2:15 I was in my solitary cell. In those few minutes I went through a heavy emotional ordeal. I had to strip down while a female guard thoroughly searched my body. I felt humiliated. I was put through everything from fingerprinting to the issuing of prison clothes. Each step inside the prison made me realize that everything was being taken away from me, including my own sense of dignity. A guard escorted me to Dorm C, where I went through the same process of stripping down and undergoing a thorough body search.

The officer in charge treated me as kindly as possible under the limitations of the system. She explained what I could expect. She assured me, "After the first few days, you'll get used to the routine around here. Then it won't be so hard on you."

I was put in an end cell that, like all the others, contained four bunks. "No one else," the officer said, "will ever occupy the cell with you."

I didn't realize it then, but for the next four and a half years, my world would consist of a room ten feet by ten feet, with bars for two sides and concrete walls for the other two. Little natural light penetrated the cell. Other prisoners in Dorm C could move around in an area about twenty feet by ten, in front of our row of cells.

I couldn't see the woman in the cell next to me because of the concrete wall between us, but we could hear each other.

"Hi, there," she said. "Don't let it get you down. The first few days are always the hardest." Hearing the sound of another human who understood what I was going through comforted me.

I had arrived in December, and she had been on death row since September. "It's going to be hard, but you'll adjust."

For the next few days she answered my questions and explained anything I didn't understand. "You'll get a physical at the hospital, and the people from mental health will be over to talk to you. You'll get a visit from the chaplain." She also told me how to set up my visitor's list of people who could come to see me. She told me that everything I had brought in with me, except a few things like my Bible, would have to be sent home. I could have my own personal lingerie and shoes, but no other clothing, not even toilet articles. I had brought two hairbrushes with me but couldn't keep them.

A guard led me out of my cell every day for one hour of exercise. Aside from that daily hour and occasional trips to the administrative building or to the mental health unit or when I was taken to court, I never moved outside of my cell for four and a half years.

My cell had a commode and a sink. A rope line stretched across the empty space dividing the two sets of bunks that were pushed against the walls. I was allowed to put up a sheet to block me from full view when I wanted to use the toilet. When I went behind that sheet and didn't come back out quickly, though, the guard on duty called my name in order to make sure I had not gone back there to hurt myself.

Four cells bordered mine to the left. A thick wall of concrete separated these cells from five more behind, all alike. When women first came into the prison, they went into those cells while being processed. Most of them stayed less than a month.

Dorm C's shower room consisted of three concrete walls, one of which held four showerheads. The room had no stalls, no doors, and no privacy. All of us stood in the open room while we showered. Some of the women brought in for processing had venereal and other contagious diseases. Sometimes I had to go behind them, and that worried me.

Leaving the shower, we could look into the only mirror in the place, a plastic one nailed to the wall. Nothing was allowed in our cells that could be used to harm ourselves.

Because Dorm C is mostly metal and concrete, sound bounced off the walls and hit the ears with a muffled roar. Women shouted constantly. A human cage.

The TV set and a table were right in front of my cell, and the only privacy I had was when I went behind the sheet. Sometimes I went back there and sat on the toilet to get away from the eyes of other people. When the guard called my name, I answered. As long as I answered, I got left alone.

The hardest adjustment involved not seeing my family. They could come on weekends once I was allowed to have visitors. I missed them, and many nights as I went to sleep, my eyes were full of tears and my heart felt as if it were breaking. I whispered prayers to God for their safekeeping.

I started having visitors by my first Saturday, any time between noon and 4:00, for up to two hours.

Another difficult adjustment involved the breakup of routine. I got used to the routine. But it seemed that as soon as I adjusted to the regularity of the schedule, something disrupted it.

Without warning, guards came to Dorm C. "Barfield, you're wanted in administration." Or I'd barely get back to

the cell when another guard came. "Barfield, to the hospital."
I never had any warning. A guard appeared, called my name,
and said, "Let's go."

My days were easier when everything went as scheduled
with no interruptions. Each morning I planned my day carefully, deciding how I would spend each half hour. A radical
change of schedule upset me. I suppose that's because the way
I spent my time was one of the few choices I had. When outside forces changed even that, I often found myself frustrated,
especially during those first few weeks of imprisonment.

Day and night the screaming kept up all around me. I had
thought the language was bad during my four months' pre-
vious imprisonment, but I had never heard anything so bad
as what I heard in Dorm C. The other ladies were "on disci-
plinary" for disobeying orders on the grounds.

After I had been there a few days, one woman began to
beat on her metal bunk and cry with a pitiful wail. She kept
that up for a solid eighteen hours.

One time lice were discovered on one woman (other prisoners called them "crabs"). I had never seen one before. But
because of that one woman, all of us had to leave our cells,
strip, and have our bodies and cells deloused. It was degrad-
ing.

I found little comfort at first. Even though I read my Bible
and prayed, I kept thinking, *How can anyone survive in this
hellhole? How can a person retain her sanity day after day?* I
prayed more fervently.

Dear God, I must have prayed dozens of times daily, *how
can I keep on taking this? I need help if I'm going to survive.*

15.

RECONCILIATION

When I arrived at prison, I was asked if I had a minister to visit me. I didn't, and so the Reverend Tommy Fuquay from the Pentecostal church in Raleigh was assigned to me. For six months he visited regularly, talking to me and praying with me.

I liked Brother Fuquay. He had an open personality and tried to help me all he could. He left Raleigh to become the pastor of a church in Stanley, North Carolina. Just before he left in midsummer 1979, he brought in the Reverend Hugh Hoyle to see me. "I thought you might like to have Brother Hoyle as your minister."

Before I had a chance to say anything, he quickly added, "Now don't feel you have to accept him as your minister."

I liked Hugh Hoyle immediately. He became my pastor for the next three years. At times of distress or confusion, he brought comfort to me. He talked often about forgiveness and how we need to ask people to forgive us the wrongs we have done toward them. I needed to hear those words.

Just as I sought forgiveness from God, I had to seek forgiveness from the people I had wronged. But more than *needing* to do it, I *longed* to do it. I knew that if I didn't attempt reconciliation with my victims' families, I would be sidestepping barriers to the peace I sought.

Up until my conversion, it had seemed that no one wanted to understand me; worse, that no one even cared. Since my conversion, however, it seemed that people were friendlier. I guess people sensed the new me, and they enjoyed my company. What a wonderful change from my old life—people actually cared about me. And I truly cared about them.

Even though I felt good about God and me, I had more than "feeling good" to let me know I was on the right track. My Bible study was an exciting discovery about the miracle of salvation. Every time I opened my Bible, it seemed as if a new insight popped off the page. My life—which for so many years had been little more than drug-dazed survival—took on a new purpose. In the beginning, I was more grateful than anything. But the more Scripture I read, the more my gratitude turned to love. If I had heard someone talking about loving God a few years ago, I would have shrugged it off. How could I understand "loving God" if I didn't know Him?

The wonder of my new life was that it wasn't anything I *did*; my new life was simply a miracle. And thank God for that, because it would be impossible to do enough good to overcome the bad I've done. The more I searched the Scriptures, the more I began to see and understand everything in a different way. Sometimes, I'd feel a sort of bubbly warmness inside me when I'd think about my family and friends. I tried to do things for people, little things to show them I cared. From an almost total disregard for life—my own and anyone else's who had been a problem to me—I began to know the sanctity of human life. I wept for those whose lives I had taken.

I had become more aware of the pain and hurt I had caused the families of the victims. I was sorry and had asked God to forgive me. I knew that I also had to ask the victims' families to forgive me. My lawyer advised me not to write any letters to them because "as long as we have any appeals left, I don't want them sent. It's possible that anything you say or write could be used against you in some way."

I did the only other thing I knew to do. I wrote a letter to those families. I wanted to tell them how sorry I was for all that I had done, even though I knew I could never make up for my crimes. With a copy to my lawyer, I gave the letter to Hugh Hoyle.

[*Editor's Note*: Anticipating her execution, Velma wrote two letters to the Reverend Hoyle for delivery to the family members of her victims. Not wanting to jeopardize her attorney's efforts, yet needing to ask forgiveness, she expressed the sorrow of her sins and the joy of her salvation. Anne Lotz attempted to deliver the letters after Velma's death.]

~~Wed. A.M.~~
~~May 27, 1984~~
Nov. 1, 1984

Dear Brother Hoyle,

I'm writing this letter to you for a special reason. I want you to read this to my family—that is if something happens to me that I can never talk with them face to face about it. I want to talk with them face to face, but right now I can't discuss my case with anyone because my case is in the process of appeals.

I wish so much that I could get them all together or either talk with each of them separate and explain my feelings. I love them, and they have been so supportive to me through all this trouble I've been in. Only a loving God could use a family to give the support to me like they have. Each one of them knows about my walk with the Lord. I've talked with them or either I have written to each of them and explained that I have confessed my sins to God, and I know that He has forgiven me and they know that I know and I'm truly born again—that I'm clean inside—that I am a new person in Christ. My old desires have passed away and all things have become new.

I want you to tell them (read to them) that many, many times I've wanted to talk with them but couldn't. And that I'm trying (I am) to clean up all the areas in my life that would keep me from having a clean conscience. And in order to do this I come to each one of them (this includes all the grandchildren too) asking them to forgive me of all the things I wronged them with. <u>I know I have brought deep hurt and sorrow and anguish</u> (<u>physical & mental pain</u>) to each one of them. I'm not saying <u>think</u> I have brought this on them. I'm saying <u>I know</u> I have brought this upon them. God has convicted me of how wrong my acts were, and I've asked Him to forgive me. And now I'm asking them to forgive me for all the wrong I've done to them. I pray that each one of them can find room in their hearts to forgive me and that God will bless each one of them real good each day of their lives. Please tell them that I have lifted them up before the throne of grace each day—and as I lifted them up my prayer was if there was ~~one~~ among them unsaved that they would be saved. I love them dearly.

Love in Jesus,
Velma

~~Wed. A.M.~~
~~May 27, 1984~~
Nov. 1, 1984

Dear Rev. Hoyle, my Brother in Christ,

I'm writing this letter for one special purpose—and that is for you to read it to the following families—the Edwards family, the Lee family, and the Taylor family. I may never get the opportunity to speak with them face to face (this is what I would like to do) or even talk with them on the phone. And I can't write them because my attorneys have advised me not to talk with anyone or write anyone anything concerning my case, because my case is now in the process of appeals.

I would ask a member of my family to do this but I feel that it will be better for you to do this because you and I have talked at deep depths about this. I've told you how I would like to go to these families face to face or if I couldn't do that, then talk with them on the phone; but as I stated above, at this particular time I cannot do this and something could happen that I may never get the opportunity to go to them personally. So I want you to get the message to them.

In the summer of 1978, in the Robeson county jail I came to my God in full surrender, repenting, confessing to Him that I was a sinner and I was asking Him to forgive me of my sins. As I was asking Him to forgive me, I told Him that I did believe His Son Jesus, His only begotten Son died on the cross for all my sins and that He arose from the grave that I might have ETERNAL LIFE. I know that night that He did forgive me and He has removed out of my life the bitterness, hatred, and rebellion that had engulfed my life. Since that night I have grown in my walk with the Lord a lot. I'm still growing. I know that I am truly born again. There were many times that I thought I was born again but I wasn't. I was only a church member, not truly born again. And there is a big difference in being a church member and in being truly born again. I know now I am saved, ready to meet my Lord. But when I was just a church member, I was afraid of death. Some may ask how do I know that I am truly born again. First of all I feel clean inside and now I have a new nature. The Holy Spirit indwells and fills me. For the first time in my life I can see with spiritual eyes and understand the secrets of God, hidden from the lost world. And this secret is Christ in me, the hope of glory. I have been made new; all things are new to me. Truly a miracle has taken place. I no longer have the desires for the old lifestyle and habits. I know Jesus as Saviour, have been born again to new and beautiful things. Even my hurts, disappointments, and failures now have meaning. I am in Him and have His joy.

As I stated earlier I have grown a lot in the Lord, and I know I will continue to grow each day as I study His Holy Word. In my growing I've studied a lot [with] my minister, Rev. Hugh Hoyle teaching me. One of the subjects that I've studied is Forgiveness. By studying this I've been led by God to go to people that I have wronged and ask them to forgive me.

And I'm asking you, Brother Hoyle, to get this message to the Dollie Edwards family, the John Henry Lee family, and the Stuart Taylor family. I will repeat, I would like to do this face to face but right now I can't, and if I never get the opportunity I want it read to them.

I come to them by way of letter asking them to forgive me of all the deep hurts and sorrows and heavy burdens that I know I have brought upon each one of them. Now I'm not saying I'm asking them to forgive me for all this hurt that I think I brought upon them. I'm saying I know I have brought this upon them, that I know I've placed more hurt and deep anguish—physical and mental pain—upon them than mere words could ever describe.

God has convicted me of how wrong my acts were—how I have wronged each of you, so now I come to you asking you to forgive me. I know He has forgiven me, and my heart's desire is that you will forgive me. My prayer is that God will bless each one of you real good each day of your life. I love all of you in Jesus.

Love in Jesus,
Velma

I could get medication at prison, but a lesser amount. I started to experience withdrawal symptoms, just as I had earlier at Dorothea Dix. This time I didn't ask for medication. Taking those capsules all the time had been troubling me. I don't want to blame them for what I did, but at the same time I'm convinced I never would have poisoned anyone if I hadn't been under the influence of those medications. After praying about it, I knew I had to get off medication. I didn't have enough of a mind to concentrate on anything. If I had one or two lucid days, for the next two or three I hardly remembered the things I had said five minutes earlier.

God, I want to serve you, and I can't without giving everything up to you. You've got to help me kick these medications. I'm willing to go through all this withdrawal if that's how it has to be. But I can't do it without you.

I had a peace about it, even though I knew that the days ahead would be hard on me. But I determined to stick it out. I memorized Hebrews 13:5, 6 and quoted the verses often, " 'I will never leave you nor forsake you.' So we may boldly say: ' The LORD is my helper; I will not fear. What can man do to me?' "

16.

SPIRITUAL SUPPORT

Because of my status, I could not attend church services. During my first week at the Correctional Center for Women, another prisoner told me about an elderly couple that came three Sundays each month and taught Sunday school for those who could not go to the chapel.

They did not come my first Sunday, but the second Sunday, just before Christmas, they came to Dorm C. Sam Roane, tall, broad, and blue-eyed with thinning white hair, was accompanied by Gales, his smiling, gray-haired wife. They gathered the women together in the open space in front of my cell. Even though I had turned to Jesus Christ, I didn't know much, and I didn't have any interest in hearing their lesson.

Sam tried to talk to me and I must have mumbled something. He assumed an indifference on my part. That may have been partly true, but I couldn't keep my thoughts together enough to figure out what he said. He handed me a lesson leaflet, just as he did to the other prisoners, even though I sat behind the bars of my cell and the others didn't. He and Gales taught the lesson. They tried, really tried, to make me feel like part of the class, but they didn't succeed.

I had not yet realized how badly I needed spiritual support. I'm thankful they kept coming back. Week after week, Sunday after Sunday, they returned. Always smiling, always showing that they cared.

"If you want to grow," Sam said Sunday after Sunday, "get into a Bible study group."

I found out later that Sam had been a successful businessman and a member of the Presbyterian church in Greensboro when he and Gales got interested in prison work. Sam retired in 1961 so that he could devote as much time as possible to helping people like me. The Roanes own a home at Myrtle Beach along the coast, but they keep a small apartment in Raleigh so they can come up every weekend to work with the prisoners.

The Roanes met me at the time I had barely started my drug withdrawal program. Each day I asked the Lord, "In my feeble way I plead for your help. Give me the strength to make it through one more day."

During the week the Roanes wrote me and let me know they thought of me every day. They knew I could win, and they kept reminding me, "God won't leave you or forsake you."

For the first six weeks, the pain was so bad that if anyone had offered me any kind of medication, I probably would have taken it. Fortunately, no one did.

I was determined to rid my system of drugs forever. Some days I did well, and other days I felt as if I had just started the battle. Somehow I kept on. The withdrawal pains stayed with me for months. It took a full year before my system was fully cleared.

When I realized I no longer had those awful reactions, I thanked God over and over that I had no more days of fuzziness. I knew what was going on in my world. Afterward— even though I had two or three days at a time when I couldn't concentrate or couldn't sleep at night—I knew that because of God's help I had won.

Worse than the withdrawal symptoms were the nightmares. I dreamed of the people I had poisoned and relived the awfulness of what I had done. In the dreams I couldn't detach myself the way I had when I had the medications in my system to deaden human reasoning and compassion. I relived everything in those nightmares, horrified at the deeds I had done.

One time I dreamed of my mother. When I awakened, her presence was so real, as if she sat in the room with me. I talked to her and begged her, "Mama, please forgive me. Forgive me for what I did to you." God had forgiven me, and I pleaded with Mama to forgive me.

After a few minutes I had a sense of peace that, if Mama knew what I had done, she had forgiven me.

That year seemed never to end. Not only was adjusting to life in prison difficult, but also adjusting to the fact that I might never walk out of that prison. In the beginning, expectations were high that my sentence would be commuted to life imprisonment. North Carolina historically has had a higher than average rate of commutations from the death sentence— actually, the highest in the nation on pre-1970 cases. Since the new death penalty in 1976, however, no one's sentence has been commuted.

If I had not been assured of Christ's love, I couldn't have survived. As I saw the sin-sickness (which is what I call it) of my soul, only God's presence kept me from taking my own life. Even so, at times I still wanted to die. I felt like Cain in the Bible who cried out to God after he had killed his brother, "My punishment is greater than I can bear!" (Gen. 4:13).

I don't know what I would have done without Sam and Gales Roane. Their faithfulness on Sunday and their letters during the week encouraged me and reminded me of their love and God's love. They became my ministers after Brother Hoyle moved. But Sam and Gales became even more. They became my teachers. Their gentle spirit and firm beliefs were water to my thirsty spirit. They refused to let me succumb to the temptations of pessimism and doubt. They taught me how to pray and how to give up my worries to God. Their insistent compassion became living witness to the truth of their words, and my swelling faith yearned to learn more and more.

I stayed in Dorm C for four and a half years. By September

1983 a new building was completed, and I was moved into it. I remained there until June 1984. For the first time I had some freedom of movement.

I couldn't leave the building, but I could walk into the dayroom. At 8:00 every morning, a guard came around and unlocked my cell. I had access to anywhere in that building until 9:00 P.M. I found myself rejoicing constantly and giving thanks to God for being able to move around and to talk freely with people.

The ceilings were low, and the noise was a kind of rumble all through the building because no acoustical material absorbs the sound, exactly like Dorm C. The mental patients were moved to the cells behind me. Some of those women beat the doors, metal cabinets, and tables and screamed all through the night. Many nights I couldn't sleep because of their noise.

In June, the superintendent, Ms. Jennie Lancaster, asked me, "Margie, (which is what everybody in prison called me), would you like to move back to Dorm C?"

I hated the thought of having only a single hour of movement, but I also knew that remaining in the new building only wore me down.

"If you go back," she said, "it won't be as difficult for you as before. I'll have to keep you locked up all day, but I can let you have free movement within the building from 5:00 P.M. until 8:00."

I agreed. When she took me back to Dorm C, it was a relief. Most of the time no other prisoners stayed in the building with me. I could rest. Others were brought in from time to time. However, once we reached the end of my appeals, Ms. Lancaster explained that since the Correctional Center had no actual death row like Central Prison (the men's prison), regulations from the state had come down that no other prisoners would live in Dorm C with me. At first they put me back into my old cell. Later, they painted and fixed up the cell at the far end of the building—it had a kind of L-shape to it. That became my home. Until 5:00 in the afternoon I stayed in my little ten by ten, but after that I could move around in a small room with a TV set and a writing table.

As a growing Christian, I had been learning to be thankful for what I had. Ms. Lancaster's presence made it obvious that she would put up with no rule breaking. Yet she had gone out of her way to treat me with every consideration she could and still remain within her duties. I never expected to see the compassion that she showed me. She tried hard to make life as pleasant for me as possible.

Of all the things for which I can thank her, the way she treated my family stands out most. She reached out to Kim especially. Even though she's not a whole lot older, she treated Kim like a daughter. She talked to her, comforted her, and often spent a few minutes preparing her to visit me and then sitting down with her afterward.

Phillip Carter, who started as an intern a month before I came to the prison, became the chaplain. He visited often, and I learned to love him. Perhaps because of his duty as a chaplain I expected that kindness, but he didn't disappoint me. When I hit low points, he unfailingly knew how to say the right words to help. More than once tears filled his eyes as he talked with me.

One particular time I felt angry toward the prison system (I don't recall the particular incident that set me off), and Chaplain Carter came by right then. He listened while I told him everything. The intensity of his dark eyes and of his whole facial expression showed me that he really listened. When I finished he patted my shoulder. "Margie, I get mad about some of those things, too."

That may not sound like much, but he understood—and he didn't lecture me. That day I didn't need a lecture.

The Roanes talked to me about a systematic and daily study of the Bible and prayer.

"Spend as much time in the Word as you can," Sam's voice boomed. "That's where you'll find strength for these bad times here in prison."

They taught me how to study and, over a period of months, I also saw the value. It reached the place where I could actually tell that on days when I spent a lot of time in prayer and study, my whole day was different. Those days when I had countless interruptions and little time alone with God, I had trouble handling the pressures.

I worked out a schedule for myself. I arranged with the guards to call me every morning at 3:00. From then until 6:00 became my truly quiet time. No interruptions. No one wanting to talk. No one coming to Dorm C with a message that I was wanted in administration.

One of my visitors commented about the hardship of getting up so early, but I told him, "My Lord deserves my best. My mind is rested, I'm alert. It's the best time of my day."

In my schedule, at 6:00 A.M. I ate and cleaned up. By 8:00 I was by my radio and had it tuned to a gospel station in Raleigh. I had a regular schedule of programs I listened to:

8:00 The Haven of Rest
8:30 Dr. John MacArthur
9:00 Dr. J. Vernon McGee
9:30 Back to the Bible
10:00 Evangelist Oliver B. Green
11:00 Chuck Swindoll
11:15 Dot Worth, a Bible teacher from New Jersey

During the week at 7:00 P.M., I listened to Dr. Charles Stanley from the First Baptist Church in Atlanta. I also heard him Sunday afternoons at 1:30 and saw his TV program on Sunday evenings.

On Sundays on TV I also watched Dr. James Kennedy, a Presbyterian minister in Florida. On our local radio station I heard Dr. Ben Haden from Chattanooga and Dr. Billy Graham.

Each weekday morning I saturated my mind in listening to the best in gospel teaching and preaching. I needed it to help me endure those days in prison.

Most afternoons I wrote letters. Over the years so many people had corresponded with me here in prison that it took all that time to keep up with the letters.

Occasionally I got caught up or didn't feel like writing, so I crocheted. I usually crocheted when I listened to all those programs in the morning, too.

I received a few letters from people who told me they were opposed to capital punishment, and I also got a few hate letters. Most of my mail came from people who wrote things such as, "I've heard of you and of what God has done in your life. I'm praying for you."

Two of the people with whom I had the most wonderful correspondence were Susie Wise and Ruth Graham. Those two women, of all the wonderful people who wrote me, seemed to know just when I needed a lift or a word of encouragement. No matter how down I got, they always wrote something to lift me up. I could never tell my story without including them.

Susie Wise, who lives in Orlando, Florida, wrote to Chaplain Ray and asked, "How can I help you with your prison ministry?"

He sent a long list of names and said she could write to any of them. He told of the loneliness of many prisoners who never hear from their families and have no friends on the outside. He included my name on that list.

Susie later told me of her reluctance to get close to me. She knew about my impending execution, and she was concerned that she might become emotionally involved and then have to struggle with the reality of my death.

However, in the summer of 1979, Susie wrote me a sweet and friendly letter. I particularly remember she said, "I'm a Christian and I'm concerned. I want you to know that you're on my prayer list, and I would like to correspond with you." From then on, the letters went back and forth between us.

For Christmas, she sent me a huge box of goodies—just

about everything the prison permitted us to have: candies, cake, nuts, gum, hot chocolate, tea, instant soups, and fruit.

She also wrote that she planned to visit the mountains of North Carolina with a friend. "If I get into your area of North Carolina, would there be any way I could visit you?"

I wrote back and explained the procedure she had to go through. In March 1980 she made her first visit. After that she made it a point to visit me at least twice a year. I had access to a pay phone, and several times I received permission to call her, since she could not call in.

It touched me that God reached several hundred miles away to Orlando, Florida, to send Susie to bring comfort and peace into my life.

In 1981 I read an article in the Raleigh newspaper about Billy and Ruth Graham. The article centered on their family life. Dr. Graham gave his wife a lot of credit for raising their children almost alone because of his frequent trips. That article particularly touched me because of the emphasis on the family. It made me realize how wonderful a Christian home can be.

After reading it, I sat down and wrote to Ruth Graham. I particularly mentioned that I would have loved to have had a family like that when I was growing up.

To my surprise, Ruth Graham personally answered my letter, and we corresponded from then on.

I am also grateful to her daughter, Anne Lotz. Anne lives in Raleigh. Through her mother's mentioning me, she wrote and later came to see me.

Anne radiates a joyfulness. When she visited me the first time in the summer of 1984, I loved her immediately. Although different, she's also much like her mother. I opened my heart to Anne in a way I had not been able to do with another woman. I decided that I would like Anne to be there at the end. I have received so much strength and love from her.

17.

"MAMA MARGIE"

Fifteen years old and sentenced to thirty years. That's the first thing I learned about Beth. When I first met her, she looked like such a child. She was, but she had been tried and convicted as an adult.

Before Beth was brought in on Saturday morning, January 24, 1981, Jennie Lancaster came over to see me. "Margie, I have a mission for you."

I wondered what she had in mind.

"Right this minute they are bringing in a young lady, fifteen years old. She's too young to be on the grounds, so we plan to put her on lockup." (That meant she would live in Dorm C where I was and have restricted privileges.) "We're putting her in the cell next to you. I want you to spend as much time talking to her as you can."

"I'm happy to help," I answered.

"You can imagine what this young lady is going through," Ms. Lancaster continued, "how lonely and confused she must feel, especially facing that kind of sentence."

I could imagine. Fifteen years old. Daddy hadn't even allowed me to date boys at that age.

They brought Beth in that afternoon. The moment I saw her, my heart went out to that child. Ms. Lancaster had not needed to ask me to spend time with Beth. I would have done it on my own. As much as I could, I tried to treat her the way

I would have wanted someone to treat my Kim. From the first day, Beth and I talked, often for hours.

In prison, most of us never asked, "What are you in for?" We associated with the same people day after day, and eventually they told us what they wanted us to know about their past, or else we learned through prison gossip. So I never asked about her past.

We talked a lot from cell to cell, but when we saw each other during our single hour of daily exercise, Beth opened up and really told me about herself. It didn't take long to realize that, at fifteen, she had been through an awful lot in life.

Beth had grown up in the western part of North Carolina. Her parents divorced when she was eight, and she lived with her mother. She did not get along with her mother.

Beth became a loner at school, and finally she skipped school as much as she attended. Often she would act as if she was getting ready for school until her mother left for work. Then she would spend the day on the streets. Beth quit school in the seventh grade. She also ran away from home for a month in the late summer of 1979.

Her restlessness and search for belonging eventually led to criminal behavior—and a thirty-year sentence when she confessed her presence at the scene of a man's murder. Because of the seriousness of the offense, she had been tried as an adult.

Superintendent Jennie Lancaster said to her, "Because of your age, we cannot put you with the prison population. I'm assigning you to the cell next to Margie Barfield, an older, motherly type woman. I would like her to be your friend."

After the administrative work of fingerprinting, stripping, and issuing prison clothing, guards escorted Beth to Dorm C. Still overwhelmed by the whole experience, Beth could hardly take in everything that happened to her that day. By evening, reality had sunk in, and she could no longer hold back the tears.

I thought of that child in the cell next to me, not old enough to be on her own, and I prayed for God to give me words of comfort for her. I didn't know what to say as I heard the pitiful sobbing.

"Beth, honey, what's wrong?"

"Nothing," she said between sobs. "Everything."

I talked to her a few minutes, but nothing seemed to help. Finally I put my hand through the bars. "Can I pray for you?"

Beth clasped my hand with a strength that made me realize how frightened and alone she felt in that cell. I would have given anything if I could have gone in there with her.

"Beth, the Lord will look out for you." I remember saying that before I prayed.

When I finished praying, that child poured out her heart to me. Soon both of us were crying. But some of her tears showed relief that she had someone near her, someone to talk to.

In the next weeks, we learned almost everything about each other. I began to think of her as my daughter, and she referred to me as her mother. It was like that, too, because we helped each other. She listened to me, returned my love, and made life much more bearable for me.

Beth made no pretense of being a Christian, but I kept talking to her about Jesus Christ. When the Roanes came for their weekly services, I urged her to attend. She could participate in those and did. The Roanes loved her immediately and showed her such deep compassion—but then, they treated everyone that way.

Beth laughingly told people, "How could I not become a born-again Christian? Margie worked on me every day, the Roanes preached to me every week, and Margie made me listen to those religious programs several hours every day."

One day Beth talked about her home life and her mother. When I said something about her father, Beth answered, "He doesn't know I'm in prison."

"Why don't you tell him?"

"I thought I'd write and tell him I've got a job and that I've moved to Raleigh."

"Don't lie to him," I pleaded with her. "Why don't you tell him the truth?"

"Because he'll blame my mother—"

"Just tell him the truth."

"I can't," she said.

The conversation ended that day. Less than a week later she brought up the matter of her father again.

"Why don't you write him?" I said. "I think he would want to know."

"You don't know my dad!"

She not only had no one but me on the inside to stand by her, she had no one on the outside. I felt so privileged to be in the cell next to her.

One night I heard her crying out in the middle of the night. I raised up and listened. She had cried in her sleep.

The next morning Beth said, "I had a terrible nightmare last night. I saw that man lying there, begging me to help him. I tried to reach out to him, but I couldn't. For some reason he was just too far away. He pleaded for help and I couldn't give it to him."

The dream recurred several times until Beth made her peace with God. She accepted the tragedy of what she had done and of her part of the crime. The poor child had so much growing up to do so quickly.

Beth and I didn't talk much about the possibility of my execution, but it worried her. I never realized how this preyed on her mind until one evening her voice came timidly from the next cell, "Margie, are they going to come and get you when I'm asleep?"

"Not that way, Beth. You'll know when I go, and I'll find some way to say good-bye to you."

"But Mama Margie, I don't want you to die—"

"It's in God's hands now, and I'm ready to go."

I meant those words because I had made myself ready. That doesn't mean it was easy or that every minute I could go around with a serene smile. Some days I cried a lot. And that night, lying in separate bunks, the lights long turned out, Beth and I both cried. I thought of our deep attachment and about leaving her behind. I worried because she still seemed so young and unable to cope by herself.

Because Beth had quit school, I urged her to study for the high school equivalency test. "You'll get out of here someday, honey," I kept telling her. "And you'll need at least a high school diploma to get any kind of half-decent job."

At the same time I worked on her, Jennie Lancaster kept writing and going through the regular channels to get Beth into a training school. According to state law, she had to be enrolled by her sixteenth birthday or she could not get in.

As Beth's sixteenth birthday approached, we made plans for a celebration. We arranged for a cake and I crocheted a gift for her.

On the afternoon before her birthday, word came through that she had been accepted in a school. The governor's office directed, "Have her there by 7:00 o'clock in the morning." The news spoiled our birthday celebration, but it provided a wonderful opportunity for Beth.

Beth left for Dillon Training School in Butner, North Carolina, on April 16, 1981, and remained there until December 15, 1982. They returned her to the Correctional Center for Women where she remained for six months. Then she went to the Cameron Morrison Youth Center in Hoffman, North Carolina, the only other prison in the state for youthful offenders. On February 9, 1984, she returned again to Raleigh.

While at the Dillon Training School, she finally wrote to her father. He wrote back immediately and came to visit her several times. During her time in Butner, he was the only visitor she had. He still remains in close contact with his daughter.

Beth had one severe blow. She had expected that, because of her age, she would get paroled when she reached twenty-one. When the board turned down her request, it automatically left her to serve a minimum of twenty years with good behavior. Beth went through a difficult time trying to accept that.

At one time she said, "I told God I wouldn't pray any more. But that didn't work either. I believe there is a God in heaven. I'm learning to trust Him to see me through all these terrible times in my life."

Beth, at nineteen, lived with the general prison population. We didn't see each other often. She worked for the canteen. Once or twice she walked over close to Dorm C, which was isolated and fenced off from the rest of the buildings. When she passed by she yelled, "Mama Margie! Mama Margie!" That's one way she had of letting me know that she hadn't forgotten her Mama Margie.

18.

INSIDE REACHING OUT

God has given me wonderful opportunities here in prison. As I've thought of the ones who have meant so much to me, I couldn't leave out Carol. She spent five or six months in the cell next to mine. We grew close to each other, and she'll always be very special to me.

Connie is another special one. When we both lived in Dorm C, a guard unlocked her cell around noon, and she would not have to go back to it until about 9:30 every night. She would pull up her chair and sit right in front of my cell so we could talk. At night she and I had Bible study and prayer together.

When I was moved to Central Prison in June 1984, I received a short letter from Connie. She wrote, "I often think of our times of Bible study and prayer and what they meant to me."

[*Editor's note:* Velma Barfield was a shy, quiet person, yet during her six years on death row, her life profoundly affected other people. In October 1984, as the time grew closer for her execution, many people who had been helped by her wanted to express their deep love and appreciation for their friend. These friends wrote letters and gave them to Chaplain Carter, who passed them on to Velma. The friends gave permission for their letters to be used in this book. The other quotations in this chapter come from printed sources, as identified.]

From Marcia:

As I reflect upon the days that we spent together in "lockup" when I first came to North Carolina Correctional Center for Women in December 1980, the pain is still as acute as it was then....I had never been locked up or in any trouble in my forty years of life. I had also never been away from my three children or my four-month old granddaughter before. Being away from them was much more overwhelming than incarceration. The pain of being uprooted from my family was more than I could bear.

I just want you to know that you helped me through the most difficult time in my life. I'm sure you recall how my sister and Mother testified against me, and the rest of the family took my sister's side against me. Until this day I never hear from my mother or any of my seven brothers and sisters....

The faith and strength that you showed me in the nine months that I was in "Dorm C" with you made all the difference in the world in how I have been able to cope with life here....I was hurt, bitter, and filled with hatred for the whole world. You changed all that for me by helping me to put all my faith in God. Because of you and being able to see you once in a while when we were being brought to visit or for counseling in the administration building, I have grown a lot in my faith in God. I still have a long way to go, but you have given me the inspiration that I needed....

I shall never forget the two of us learning to crochet together. I still have the granny-square bedroom slippers you made for me, and I shall always treasure them. I have a treasure chest full of memories of our Bible study classes and prayer sessions in front of your cell.

Margie, you have a very special place in my heart and there you shall live forever. Of this I speak for myself and many others here that have known you and loved you for so many years.

From Julie who wrote a letter to Chaplain Carter about "Miss Margie":

Margie has a naturally radiant air I never could explain. The light, nonjudgmental and warm features of her face and attitude always drew me to her. She was a safe haven to me; I could trust her to love me no matter what. She took a lot of time out for me—whether it was to listen, to talk, to give advice, or just to be there 'cause I needed her. She had a lot of abuse from staff because we weren't supposed to talk to or lean on Margie. But out of kindness and genuine concern she was there anyway. She was not negative to staff about it; they knew, as we all did, that Margie was just good. No one could deny it when her laughter would bless those dark lockup halls.

From Ellen:

I came to this prison in quite a state of shock. I was tried, found guilty, convicted, and sentenced to a life sentence for a crime that I'm not guilty of. I knew no one, trusted no one, and so I had no one to turn to. Of course I had God, but I was about to give up on Him. But you stepped into my life. No one but you seemed to take an interest in me and try to talk to me. I was simply lost.

You told me to keep trusting in God and to keep praying and He would help me and He has. God and my Bible, which you also helped me to get, that's my survival kit. At times I was rude, didn't even answer when you talked, but you didn't give up. Thank God for that.... But you helped in other ways, too. You told me how to have a decent, clean dress, about cosmetics, and a lot of other things....

I was pretty much gone, Margie. Would you believe, I even thought Chaplain Carter a maintenance man, Chaplain Jones a voodoo doctor, and preacher Roane a leader of a cult? I have come a long way since I saw you. I have really done a lot of apologizing and asked everyone to forgive me.

I have gotten a certificate from upholstery, gotten my G.E.D., and now work in canteen. I also do volunteer work in the chaplain's office....

I have made many friends here in prison. But, Margie, you are one of the best friends I could ever have. There are many, many more here that feel the same as I do....

Thank God for a woman like Margie Barfield, who has so much on her but yet has taken up so much time to help others.

In a lengthy article, "Does This Woman Deserve to Die?" that appeared in *The Village Voice* (June 1984),* reporter Elin Schoen said:

---

* Reprinted with permission of the author and *The Village Voice*, copyright © 1984.

Several of Velma's most devoted correspondents are living elsewhere in the prison, young inmates whom prison officials have placed in the cell next to hers, breaking their own rules by permitting her contact with them, knowing that Velma, just through talking with them, could help. "My adopted kids," Velma calls them. Some have been as young as 15. "That's just a baby, placed in prison, you know. And that's so hard when you see someone like that who's hurting so. I can relate so much to some of the hurt that they suffer because I have hurt, too.... I know the feeling of not even wanting the daylight to come."

Ginny Carroll, a staff writer for the Raleigh *News and Observer* and one who has followed the Velma Barfield case closely, wrote on July 1, 1984:

...the former mental health director of the women's prison said in an interview that she had considered Mrs. Barfield a "mental health resource."

"My staff and I were sometimes able to place patients [who had become disruptive] in the cell next door to Margie so that she could counsel them in the informal sense and help them achieve stable behavior," says Gretchen J. Belovicz, now a private clinical psychologist in Raleigh.

Phyllis Tyler also quoted Ms. Belovicz, in an article which appeared in the June 28, 1984, issue of *Spectator Magazine:*

Belovicz knew Velma Barfield for a year and a half while serving as Mental Health Director and Chief Psychologist at Women's Prison....

"My reactions to Margie were consistently favorable," she told me. "She is unfailingly friendly, open, polite, and 'positive' in her approach to situations. I *never* heard her complain about the conditions in which she lived even when these were strikingly bad. Despite the incredible constraints placed upon her, she always tried to fill her time constructively rather than sitting idly as so many would do.

"More important to me than her general demeanor was her extreme concern and thoughtfulness toward other inmates, many of whom exhibited depression and some of whom exhibited symptoms of very severe emotional disturbance. I think it is fair to say that Margie became an informal Mental Health 'resource,' although I do not believe that Margie was ever aware of this—or ever received any thanks for it from any of us...."

From Carol:

Let me tell you how much I appreciate you. I will never forget those days as a safekeeper, when I was so discouraged, depressed, and felt like there was no one in the world who cared.

It was your love for God that helped me open my eyes and see that I had so much to be thankful for. I can remember the day that we were allowed to sit in front of your cell and read God's Word and have prayer.

When my family was rushed out of the state and I only received a note from Mother...I will never forget how you prayed for me and the family. Many times when it was all I could do to keep my composure, you still prayed....

Margie, I just want you to know that I love you in Christ and that I'll meet you in heaven on those streets of pure gold, where there will be no sadness, no tears to dim the eye, just pure rejoicing....

From Barbara, to Mama Margie:

First of all, let me tell you I love you and miss you dearly. I really don't know how to start this letter off. There is so much that I want to tell you but trying to find the right words is very hard. I still can remember the first night I saw you. The concerned look on your face and the love in your eyes. I was scared, and I could tell you wanted to reach out to me and tell me that everything is going to be all right, that you loved me, and so did God.

Later on when they finally moved me to C Hall, little did I know just how big a part you would play in my life. I can still recall the day I spoke to you about asking God back into my life. You spoke to Sam and Gales Roane about the decision I had made. I was surprised to find out that on May 20, 1984, you had made arrangements with Sam and Gales to lead me in rededicating my life to God. But through your love and guidance I have turned my life back to God.

You have always told me that God will work out our problems and we are never alone as long as we have faith in God. Whenever I needed a shoulder to cry on about my problems, you were always there, along with a prayer for me. You always listened to our problems instead of worrying about yourself. I always enjoyed the Bible study that we used to have together. I really did need it more than I realized. I don't know if I ever did thank you or not for helping us to be able to attend Sunday school and helping us get our Bible study underway.

Mama Margie, the day they moved you from Single Cell to Dorm C, my heart was broken, but the day they moved you to Central Prison I felt like my world had ended because then I knew that I would never be able to go to the window again and let you know how much I love you and missed you. But the day you returned I felt like I had come back to life again. You have been like a second mother to me. You were always there when I needed someone by talking to me about God. I have faith in Him....

Susan writes:

I just want you to know that I love you and miss you with all my heart. I remember all the times you talked to me about God.... Your words are like an echo in my mind that I can listen to when I am lonely, depressed, or frightened. I will never forget you. You were there when my faith in God was weak and I was very shaken. But through you and our conversations about the Lord, I found strength and peace. I always wondered how you could manage a smile, even in the face of death. It was too much for my mind to grasp. I never asked you, but instead I observed you. You always spoke of God and His greatness. And how He is in complete control even when we don't realize it....

I know you are very close to our God. I can hear it in the things you say, and I can see it in your actions. How many times have you told me, "God is my rock"? It showed in the warmth of your smile and in the time you gave so unselfishly helping us girls learn to crochet.

You always said that no matter what we do here in prison, stay in the Word of God. That was the best advice that we could have gotten, and at a time when we all needed something to hold on to. Especially me.... My whole world had collapsed around me. I sincerely thought that God had deserted me. But you kept reminding me that was not true and that God cares about me and knows what I'm going through. And you said that I should trust in Jesus. I have done that very thing, and now He is my rock and I love Him with all my heart.... I shudder to think of what would have happened to me if you had not been there to remind me that God is real and He loves me and cares about me....

I want you to know that I am seriously considering the ministry and you are a big part of that decision. You taught me many things about God, and I just want to thank you for your words of wisdom, your love, and support you gave me when no one else seemed to care. And also for the wonderful, beautiful memories that I will cherish forever and ever....

19.

THE LAST APPEAL

The original date set for my execution was February 3, 1979. I never thought of that date as final because my attorney, Bob Jacobson, made it clear that we had an automatic appeal process to go through.

Bob had been appointed by Robeson county to be my attorney when I went to trial. Although a nice and friendly man, he had never tried a capital-offense case before. During the trial Bob asked for assistance, but the judge turned him down.

Bob went through the case with me without really knowing me, and I didn't cooperate—not because I didn't want to help, but at the time I was on such heavy medication that I hardly knew what was happening.

In North Carolina they have an automatic appeal for capital-offense convictions. Bob got help in making the appeal in the person of Richard (Dick) Burr III, who worked with a private foundation called the Southern Prisons Defense Team (he is now with the West Palm Beach Public Defenders' Office).

The defense at the trial had been "Not guilty by reason of insanity." I don't blame my attorney. I hadn't cooperated—I hadn't been fit to cooperate—but he did almost nothing to prove that because of heavy doses of medication, I had committed the crimes without having the ability to reason what I had done.

After reading the complete trial transcript, Dick decided that in making an appeal on my behalf, he would also cite incompetency of counsel, and so he suggested that Bob resign. Bob did resign. He really wanted to help me.

Dick appealed to the United States Supreme Court. They refused to hear the case. The state set a September 1980 date for my execution. At the time, Dick Burr lived in Tennessee. By North Carolina law, a state-certified attorney had to make the appeal for a stay of execution. Dick contacted James (Jimmie) D. Little, in Fayetteville at the time, now in Raleigh. After studying the trial proceedings, Jimmie agreed to represent me in asking for a stay of execution.

I started keeping a journal about the end of 1980. I didn't write in it every day, but I did try to record the events and feelings that touched me the most. The entries dealing with appeals read like this:

> Getting prepared for the post-conviction hearing was another dark time for me—working with Mr. Little meant that I would have to start all over again—going back as far as I could remember, telling him all about myself and the crimes.
>
> Just thinking about this depressed me but I remembered the trials Job suffered, holding fast to God's hand. I remembered, too, the Scripture verses Hebrews 13:5, 6; Matthew 28:20; and Isaiah 41:10, 13. I needed my Divine Helper, God's Divine Presence and His Divine Hand to hold mine.

> In the days ahead preparing for the post-conviction hearing and for the week in court for this, fear and depression (Satan himself!) tried to paralyze me, but I found comfort in knowing that in days of shattering defeat, God was there with me. I recognized His presence and learned how to rely on His power by committing my way (Psalm 37:5) to the Lord instead of worrying over the hearing and the preparation. I trusted God to hold fast to my hand and to lead me safely through all my trials.

> It would have been easier...for God to remove the pain I would suffer through the post-conviction hearings, but again God knew what I needed, and so He let me go through all of

this—to stay in the pain—endure the criticism again so that He could teach me that He was there waiting to help me *in* it and to bring me *through* it. He didn't give a guarantee He would take me out of the hard places, but He promises me grace whenever I need it.

We were in court [for the post-conviction hearing] all week, Monday through Friday, and then the judge didn't rule until the following Wednesday. He ordered me held over in the county jail.... There were a number of ladies there in the jail. Each morning two of them joined me in Bible study and prayer!

On the following Wednesday, I appeared in court at 2:30 P.M. to hear Judge Braswell's decision. He ruled against me and set another execution date in December. [It was then November 1980.] I was transferred back to [the] women's prison—back to the same cell.

Needless to say, I was disappointed. I knew my times (Psalm 31:15) were in His hand, and in my days of weakness, God's grace would be sufficient for me. It was another one of those times that fear tried to grip me, so when I'm afraid I will trust.

The next years were years of waiting. The December date was set. The North Carolina Supreme Court denied the appeal to hear my case. I was taken to Whiteville, North Carolina, for this hearing—for a date to be set. I was brought back to the prison that afternoon. My attorneys again had to file a petition asking for this execution date to be removed. The stay came about two weeks later, and my attorneys filed with the North Carolina Supreme Court asking them for a new trial or for my sentence to be commuted. The court ruled against me. That was in December. So the district attorney ordered me back to court for another execution date to be set. I had to appear in court on Tuesday before Christmas, in Elizabethtown, and the execution date again was set. My attorneys filed asking this date to be removed until they had time to file again in the North Carolina Supreme Court.

After the North Carolina Supreme Court refused to consider the case, my attorneys filed in the Eastern District Federal Court in Raleigh. The judge heard oral arguments and later denied relief. We went through the same process at the Fourth Circuit Court of Appeals, a federal appeals court, in Richmond, with the same result. After the U.S. Supreme Court denied relief in the spring of 1984, my attorneys asked for reconsideration by that court. Chief Justice Warren Burger granted a stay of execution that was dissolved in August 1984. The District Attorney ordered another execution date to be set. It was set for August 31.

Jimmie explained to me very early, "We have not completed the routes available to us in court." He helped me realize that we had a lot of paths still open to us and that we should not regard any date as final.

I had understood so little during the trial because of the fuzziness of my mind. When Jimmie Little got involved, he patiently explained each step to me. If Jimmie thought I didn't understand anything, he went over it until I grasped it. He carefully traced the steps of appeal we would go through. As he explained, when one court denied an appeal, we would go to the next. Jimmie started working with me in September of 1980, right after the state Supreme Court refused to hear our appeal.

I felt discouraged when I heard the news, but Jimmie told me, "Velma, it will take years before we finally get this case settled. First we go through the entire appeal system. And if nothing comes of that, we'll ask for clemency."

Basically, a prisoner can appeal through the lower courts three times to the U.S. Supreme Court. The first two times we went by way of the state courts and the third by federal courts. It all takes time and a lot of work on the part of the lawyers.

Slowly, or so it seemed to me, the appeals went to the proper courts. In every instance, they refused to hear our case. That never stopped Jimmie and Dick. They just went to work on the next step.

After the U.S. Supreme Court had rejected pleas twice, and the Fourth U.S. Circuit Court of Appeals also rejected our plea on October 3, 1983, they then filed a request before the U.S. Supreme Court for a review of the case.

Since the original date of February 3, 1979, three other dates of execution had been set: October 17, 1980; December 12, 1980; and March 22, 1982. In each instance, I had received a stay of execution.

When the U.S. Supreme Court refused to hear our case for the third time and Judge Robert L. Farmer set August 31, 1984, as my date of execution, I had a sense of finality. I realized that the years Jimmie had talked about were coming to an end. Until that August 31 date, I knew we always had another chance to appeal.

I thanked Jimmie, knowing he had done his best. I thought of his involvement in my life. We had grown so close over the past four years. He's a fine lawyer, but it goes far beyond that. He got no money for what he'd done in my case. I couldn't begin to imagine the time and cost on his part. He'd made a hundred trips to the prison to see me.

"You've done everything you could, Jimmie."

Tears filled his eyes. "We're not licked yet, Velma. We're not giving up now."

I heard the words, but in my heart I didn't think too seriously about them. As far as I could understand, we had reached the end, and I could see nothing up ahead.

In my cell that evening, I thought, *The wait of six years will soon be over.* I didn't feel any sense of fear, but I knew that the closer we got to the execution, the more difficult it would be for me, and especially for my family. Over and over I prayed, *Lord, give me strength to endure these last days.* Even as I prayed, I knew God would.

I wrote to Ruth Graham at that time: "If I am executed on August 31, I know the Lord will give me dying grace, just as He gave me saving grace, and has given me living grace."

On Wednesday, June 20, almost two and a half months before my scheduled execution, the order came to move me to Central Prison. I had thirty minutes to get ready. I grabbed my Bible and a letter I had received that morning from Ruth

Graham. Mostly I stood paralyzed and angry as I watched a guard dump my belongings in a large plastic bag, the kind they use for garbage. Seeing my pictures, wall posters, and printed Scripture plaques all going into the plastic bag made me think that, in a sense, that's what it must have meant to the guards, getting rid of things and tidying up. But to me the objects they tossed inside the plastic represented the past six years of my life. Helplessly, I stood there, reminding myself they were only doing their duty. I had to stop looking because it hurt so much.

When they finished and I prepared to walk out of the cell, I thought, *Nothing shows I've ever been here or that I ever existed. Nothing here will tell the next person about the wonderful times of fellowship I shared with the Lord.* I wished I could have left a poster or a book—something for the next prisoner—to communicate God's love to her when she enters this cell.

On the way to Central Prison, which took only ten minutes because it was only about two miles away, I re-read Ruth Graham's letter to ease my mind and to prepare myself for the ordeal that lay ahead. Her letter gave me such an uplift. Here is part of that letter:

> What would we do without Him? How could we carry on without the joy of His companionship? The indescribable relief and comfort of His forgiveness?
>
> God has turned your cell on Death Row into a most unusual pulpit. There are people who will listen to what you have to say because of where you are.
>
> As long as God has a ministry for you here, He will keep you here. When I compare the dreariness, isolation and difficulty of your cell to the glory that lies ahead of you, I could wish for your sake that God would say, "Come on Home."
>
> ...How good of God to meet us where we are. And because of Him, you and I are sisters. Let's pray for one another as well as for our children.
>
> Thank you for the blessing you have
> been to me. And may He reach many of
> the other women there through your
> loving, faithful witness to His mercy.

The early move to Central Prison surprised me and everyone else. Usually, prisoners are moved to death row about seventy-two hours before the execution. This was more than two months prior to the execution date.

Everything was totally different at Central. I had come to know the guards at the women's prison. Some of them I called friends, even though we carefully kept the line clear between prisoner and guard.

When I reached Central, they stripped me down, searched me, and handcuffed me as they walked me to death row. My cell had no windows. I couldn't tell daylight from night except by my watch or the changing of shifts. Every fifteen minutes a guard appeared to check on me. Seconds later I could hear him report something like, "2:00 check, Barfield reading."

At the women's prison, at times I had other ladies in the same building, but at Central I had no one anywhere around me. Officers kept coming and going or shifts changed, but otherwise I was shut off from the rest of the world.

The worst part of living on death row was that they placed me in the cell next to the gas chamber. Every time I got called out of my cell for any purpose, I had to walk past that room. Even sitting in my cell I could look out and see it.

The light in my cell burned constantly, day and night. I was restless anyway, and with the light burning, every time I turned over, I awakened. I finally asked if the amount of light could be cut down at night while I slept. I didn't expect it to be cut off and didn't even ask. By the second week, when I decided to go to sleep, the lights were dimmed for me.

As soon as I got up in the morning, the guard turned up the light, and it stayed bright until I went to bed at night.

I faced totally different living conditions from what I had been used to. When they took me down to see my attorney, someone had parked a hospital gurney outside the gas chamber. The next time I went down, the gurney was still there, although eventually they removed it.

I don't know why they put the gurney there. Maybe they thought I would have complications, or try to kill myself—I don't know how I could have—and they would have to rush me to the hospital. I know they kept prepared in case I tried to kill myself.

Going to Central had to be one of the lowest points in my life since I had become a Christian. I had nothing—no privacy, no sense of dignity, no one near me. I felt absolutely helpless.

I had visitors, but I had to go through a lengthy process first. I was stripped and searched before and after each visit. A guard handcuffed me while we walked to and from the visit. I could talk to visitors only with a glass partition between us.

Fortunately, after a week, they stopped searching me on the way down. I still underwent a complete body search after each visit. I don't know how I could have gotten access to anything because I never came into physical contact with anyone.

They placed me in a holding cell, one of four. A guard told me that James Hutchins, executed at Central Prison on March 16, 1984, had occupied that same cell.

For the first two or three days, everything seemed a mass of confusion around me. The move from an orderly, systematic way of life had been abruptly changed to the holding cell in Central Prison. Everything was different. I saw no familiar faces. I didn't understand the strict routine and the constant supervision. I couldn't get my thoughts together. I tried to read but the words didn't mean anything.

I kept thinking about being in the same cell where James Hutchins had spent his last days. I felt so alone. A wave of depression fell over me—not depression because I faced death, but depression because I had no privacy and was being watched constantly.

In desperation, I fell on my bunk, being careful not to let my guard see tears. I didn't want him to panic and rush me over to mental health for someone to shove a pill at me to alleviate my depression.

With my face to the wall, and as quietly as I could, I let my tears fall. While Jesus Christ had forgiven me for everything,

I still had to bear the responsibility for the hurt I had caused. Not a day passed that I didn't think about that. Especially during those first two or three days at Central, I couldn't get past my feelings of shame. The names and faces of my victims swam before my eyes. *God, please, help me! Remove from me those things I can do nothing about.*

I quoted Isaiah 26:3:

> You will keep him in perfect peace,
> Whose mind is stayed on You,
> Because he trusts in You.

Gradually I relaxed. Peace came to me. I felt assured that I would learn to live on death row until either another appeal came through or they executed me.

Something wonderful happened that I find hard to explain. The presence of Jesus Christ became so real to me, I could almost see Him. I'd never had an experience as powerful as that one. He became as real to me in that cell as if Jimmie Little had stood there talking to me.

In that same cell where James Hutchins had lived out his last days, I felt as if God were speaking to my inner being.

"Velma, you prayed often for James Hutchins during his last days. I was here, right here with James. He's gone now, but I'm still here. And I'm here with you."

That knowledge snapped me out of my depressive crying and self-pity. God was with me—everywhere—that's what the Bible says, and that's what I had learned at women's prison. I now had an inner certainty that God was with me at that very moment. And I felt a special closeness to Him.

I had allowed noise and confusion to turn my mind away from Jesus Christ.

From then on, I knew I could endure until I was taken from the cell for the last time on August 31. None of us had any hope for further appeals, but it didn't matter. I was at rest.

I could read again, and everything I read gave me new strength. I had been in such deep distress, but God had given me balm for my soul.

I never expected to walk out of Central Prison, but I did. Jimmie and Dick had gotten another stay. After two weeks, they returned me to the Correctional Center for Women on July 2, 1984.

Jimmie had been working with a committee since the spring of the year to appeal for clemency. They planned to ask Governor James B. Hunt, Jr., to commute my sentence to life imprisonment. The committee had worked hard collecting information, contacting witnesses, and gathering testimonies to support a clemency appeal on the basis of my rehabilitation.

Jimmie had started to contact people who would be willing to go before Governor Hunt on my behalf. At first he had asked me to write to people. Then he and others formed a committee, the "Margie Velma Barfield Support Committee." I wrote to friends, asking if we could use their names. The committee printed letterhead stationery and a brochure, wrote hundreds of letters, contacted the media, and made a video tape.

Sister Mary Teresa Floyd, a Roman Catholic nun involved in social work at the women's prison, did so much in getting up the petition for clemency. She wrote and talked to dozens of people and spent an enormous amount of time and energy.

The brochure had my picture on the front and said, "This Woman Is on Death Row!" Below my picture, they placed the words, "A Shared Responsibility?" One of the things they wrote touched me:

> She has admitted her guilt. She is now drug free and is now painfully aware of the gravity of her actions, and there, but for the grace of God, could go any one of us.
>
> Velma Barfield cried out over a lifetime for help that never came...
>> from her friends
>> from her family
>> or from society.
>
> And yet, she does not presume, even now, to ask the state for forgiveness or freedom—just her life.

The committee talked to the media, trying to spread the information as far and as wide as possible. Journalists started contacting us for interviews. The whole news media took a new interest in my case. Two reporters in particular I recall, one from *The Village Voice* and the other from *The Los Angeles Times*, interviewed me and showed deep compassion for me.

Phyllis Tyler wrote an article titled "A Constructive Life on Death Row" for *Spectator Magazine*, June 28, 1984:

> The day Margie Velma Barfield's execution date was set, I lost my naive trust in the nightly news. I had watched two news networks, NBC and CBS, simultaneously film the story that was broadcast the day she was condemned to die. The two stories were totally different.
>
> One story emphasized the remarks of the prosecuting attorney, Joe Freeman Britt, who called her a calculating, cold-blooded killer hiding as a sweet little grandmother. "She is a dangerous woman," he said, "who should die and get it over with." A neighbor of the murdered man was shown saying she'd like to give Velma Barfield the shot herself.
>
> The other story gave the cold facts of the case, too: she had poisoned her fiance while under the influence of drugs prescribed by several physicians. She admitted to three other murders, one of whom was her mother, while she was on drugs. The newswoman quoted people who know and love Velma Barfield, as well as the prosecuting attorney. She made no excuses for Velma Barfield, but it was a sympathetic story.
>
> I was reminded of the fable of three blind men who described an elephant: one felt the trunk and said an elephant is like a snake; another a leg and said it is like a great tower; another the tail and said an elephant is like a rope.
>
> There is a Velma Barfield that the jury who condemned her to death never saw. It is a woman I have come to know very well over the past four years. I think I am intuitive about people and not easily fooled. I know her a lot better than Joe Freeman Britt, the prosecutor who is listed in the Guinness Book of Records as the deadliest in the country.

Most of the media people treated me nicely enough, but after awhile the questions repeated themselves. "What is it like in prison?" "Tell us how you spend a typical day." "What hopes do you have for clemency?" "How does all this affect your family?" "Have you had an opportunity to talk with the families of the victims?" When I told them no, they would usually ask, "If you had an opportunity what would you say to them?"

Governor Hunt had scheduled September 18, 19 to hear arguments pro and con on our plea for commutation.

I was nervous when my supporters went for the hearing. Every appeal we had made had failed, and that didn't encourage us. But more than that, I wondered if Governor Hunt would believe those who went in my defense. I knew I had changed. I knew that the Velma Barfield on death row was not the same Velma Barfield who poisoned those people.

I knew who I had become, and so did God. A few other people believed in me. But was it enough to make a difference?

20.

CLEMENCY DENIED

How do you wait for a decision that determines whether you live or die? During the jury trial, I had been so fuzzy-headed from medication, I had hardly known what was going on.

More than forty supporters appeared before Governor Hunt on Tuesday, September 18. My spirits were lifted when I saw so many whom I loved present. It meant so much to me. My children came, my four living brothers and two sisters, former inmates, pastors, and friends, including Anne Lotz.

Besides the testimony of people who told of my great change, a fifteen-minute video tape made by my support committee was shown.

My brother, Jimmy Bullard, now a minister, made a statement to the press:

> We would like for everyone to know that we love her and have forgiven her for what she has done. We know that what she is doing in prison now is helping other people—young people and older people alike.

Ronnie also made a statement that touched me deeply:

> The Velma Barfield in prison today is not the Velma Barfield who did the things that she has confessed to doing....She was

a different person [before going to prison] and had no control over her life at all.

He tried to explain about my addiction to the medications for ten years and said I "lived from pill to pill." He told them that I had given up drugs since my imprisonment and had changed dramatically.

The statement that touched me the most was:

We do not ask for forgiveness from the governor. We ask him for compassion so that she may spend her remaining years in prison, not only for us, but for our children who love their grandmother.

On the day after we made our request, those who opposed clemency appeared before the governor.

Now, six years since my trial, still living on death row, I waited for the decision by Governor Hunt. I prayed—as I had been praying all along. I had known it could go either way, and I had no clear-cut feeling about it. Jimmie tried so hard to encourage me, while at the same time wanting to prepare me if Governor Hunt turned us down.

Jimmie told me, and later elaborated for a press statement: "This is one of the most compelling cases for clemency in the United States, and genuine, explicit evidence supporting the rightness of clemency was presented to Governor Hunt."

On Thursday, September 27, a guard took me to the administration building shortly after 5:30. Ms. Lancaster told me that they had received word that the governor would meet with the press at 6:00, giving them his decision.

"Jimmie's on his way over here now to talk to you." I tried to read the expression in her face and voice but I couldn't tell if she even knew the decision.

While waiting for my lawyer, I prayed silently, *O God, cover me with Your grace. Help me. You know that, in my own human way, I want the governor to commute my sentence. Lord Jesus, for six years I've prayed for my Father's will to be done.*

Now I'm asking You to help me accept Governor Hunt's decision, whichever way he rules.

At 5:45 Jimmie walked in. Before he said anything, I knew. The expression on his face told me the decision.

"He'll be meeting with the press in a few minutes," Jimmie said, referring to the governor.

I saw the pain on his face and wanted to ease that in some way, and yet I knew I couldn't. I waited for him to tell me the rest.

Quietly he said, "The governor will be denying clemency."

For a few seconds I was quiet. I couldn't say anything. The disappointment hurt. Silently I thanked God for His grace for that moment. As I prayed, I did feel stronger and more able to cope. No more waiting. Now I knew.

I looked up at Jimmie, and tears filled his eyes. "Oh, Jimmie, you've worked so hard. You tried. No one could have done anything more—"

I don't know if he actually said, "I failed," or if that's the sense I picked up from the way he responded. "Jimmie, no one on earth could have done more than you and Dick did. You've been so wonderful to me over the years."

The governor appeared before the press saying that I must "pay the maximum penalty" for my crimes.

As part of his statement, he said:

> I have listened to supporters of Mrs. Barfield for clemency, including relatives and friends of Mrs. Barfield's victims....There is no question of her guilt....After carefully looking at the issues, I don't believe that the ends of justice or deterrence would be served by my intervention in this case....I cannot in good conscience justify making an exception to the law as enacted by our state legislature, or overruling those twelve jurors who, after hearing the evidence, concluded that Mrs. Barfield should pay the maximum penalty for her brutal crimes....

The saddest thing for us as we stayed there was that he did not respond to the issue. The appeal readily acknowledged my guilt and never made any denial. The request came because of my changed life—my rehabilitation, as they called it.

After the newscast that we listened to on radio, Jimmie spoke out angrily at the decision. I put my hand on his. "Jimmie, you can't be that way. You have to forgive him. He did what he thought best. And a lot of us have been praying for God's will. Please—don't stay angry at him."

Then I sat still for a few minutes, talking quietly to my Lord, asking for His sustaining strength. *O God,* I whispered, *I need Your comfort.* I would soon talk to both Kim and Ronnie, and I had to keep my composure.

People kept coming into the room with interruptions of all kinds. I heard words of comfort, of sorrow, of encouragement, and more interruptions. But every second possible, I asked for Him to help me when I talked to my children.

The blessed Holy Spirit began pouring His healing balm into my heart—easing some of the discomfort and stress I was experiencing, reminding me that my times were in my Father's hand (Psalm 31:15). And I just needed to be still—wait on God—trust in Him to pour His strength into me—"in quietness and in confidence shall be your strength" (Isaiah 30:15).

In my quietness I discovered anew that God was my helper and that He had never failed me. It was beautiful how God lifted the curtain of distress and disappointment and showed me His providential hand—consoling my heart (Matthew 6:33).

After a few more minutes, Ms. Lancaster placed a call to Kim for me. She was so torn up after seeing it on the news. She could hardly talk. "Oh, Mama..." she cried.

It was hard to keep my composure when I heard her crying, but God gave me strength as I tried to calm her down.

After that call, Ms. Lancaster placed a call to Ronnie. I had expected him to handle it better. He sounded as torn up as Kim. "Ronnie, we have to accept this. We've prayed and God's will is going to be done here. I don't know why it has turned out this way, but we have to accept it."

Later, back in my cell, I read the little piece, "Footprints," written by an unknown author. It helped.

One night I dreamed I was walking along the beach with the Lord. Many scenes from my life flashed before me. In each one I noticed footprints in the sand. Sometimes there were two sets but at other times there was only one. This bothered me because I noted that during periods of depression, when I was suffering from anguish, sorrow, or severe testing, I could see only a single set. So I prayed in my distress, "You promised, Lord, that if I followed You, You'd walk with me always. But I've noticed that during the most trying periods of my life, there has been just one set of prints in the sand. Why, when I needed You most, haven't you been with me?"

To which my Lord replied, "The times when only ONE set of footprints were made, my child, were the times I CARRIED you!"

After talking with my kids, I also talked with my younger sister, Fay Paul. She was so torn up that I found it hard to talk to her. Yet the Lord's strength sustained me. Or as the apostle Paul said it, "the Lord stood with me and strengthened me" (2 Timothy 4:17).

Since the denial of our plea for clemency, everything has been going on here at a rapid rate. I suppose that now we all know the end is coming. It is a time of great testing for me. I'll be having visits from family members, making funeral arrangements, talking with both attorneys—so much going on. I have to keep calling on the Lord's strength each day as I face the next step.

[*Editor's note:* The following entries come from Velma Barfield's journal as marked.]

Saturday, September 29, 1984:
Kim...and her two daughters, my precious grandchildren, visited me....Again, Kim was so broken, and I had a real struggle this time keeping my own self from pulling apart at the seams. How grateful I am that our Lord knows about our grief and sorrows! He knows every pain in whatever way it may be and stands ready to give us grace to carry our burdens.

Kim and I had some time by ourselves, and I told her as painful as all of this is, I feel God has given us a very special time—that many people never have before separating from their loved ones....

We talked about hurts that we had caused each other, and I told her the one thing that I had had a big struggle with was the pain, hurt, shame, and disgrace that I had brought to her and Ronnie and to all the others—members of my family and the victims' families. It was difficult to talk to her about all this without coming apart. In fact, I did break and cry for a bit. She cried and I cried.

She said, "Mama, please don't say that, you were there when Ronnie and I needed you."

I didn't feel I had been with them when they needed me.

Kim and I talked about my final [funeral] arrangements. That wasn't easy for either of us, and it has been the most painful visit we have had since my incarceration. After Kim left, I felt as if every fiber of my being had been torn apart.

I went back to my cell, and in the quietness there I poured out all my hurts and bruises to the Lord. He knew every pain I suffered. As I lay there, troubled over my failures to my children and how they had stood by me, I thought of that song, "I Must Tell Jesus."

I did tell Jesus my sorrows, and He removed my burdens and gave me peace. I'm still learning that in order to have peace in the midst of my circumstances, I must continually commit my way to my Lord and rest in the confidence that He will surely bring me through.

October 2, 1984:
I talked with Dr. Billy Graham and his wife Ruth on the phone. It was wonderful—uplifting—to talk with them. It encouraged me. I felt as though I was then in the heavenland.

(I have never seen the Grahams in person, but I received permission to call them. We talked for ten minutes. Before hanging up, Dr. Graham prayed for me. It was one of my best days in prison. Chaplain Carter said that I walked three inches above the ground the rest of the day.)

October 6, 1984:
Ronnie and his son Tommy visited, and I again felt depression trying to raise its ugly face. Ronnie had told me earlier, soon after he got here at 10:30, that this could be my last visit with Tommy. He felt as though his other visits should be by himself. This was painful as I talked with Tommy, knowing it could be my last visit with him. Again it was a time of praying without ceasing—silently asking God to give me strength to endure. I must admit I was feeling a bit crushed inside, and when

Tommy left (Sister Mary Teresa took him for a while) I really felt crushed, but continued to cling to God's promise—"For You are with me" (Psalm 23:4). I knew He was accompanying me, soothing my irritations and hurts with His anointing oil of love and compassion.

After Ronnie left, I wanted so much to be alone, but I had another visitor. She stayed for about an hour. Then I came back to my building and have to admit I was drained. This was another time I felt the need to be alone with my Lord and tell Him all my hurts. It's times like these that I must hide myself deep in my hiding place—in the secret place of the most high—Jesus Christ my Lord and Saviour....

21.

THE LAST DAYS

The struggle for peace demanded more of me at Central Prison than at any point in my Christian life. I finally reached the place where I could withstand the pressures around me and I could honestly say, *I am at peace with God and with myself.*

After two weeks at Central Prison, I received a reprieve—temporary, as it turned out—because Jimmie and Dick raised an issue over the jury selection. While waiting for a Supreme Court decision,* the order came to send me back to women's prison.

As strange as it may seem, I looked forward to being back at Dorm C—it had become home to me. The people who had grown closest to me over the years were there, too. Nothing, I decided, would ever be as bad as going back to Central Prison.

Going back meant two months longer to live. And then what? I kept praying, *God, You have seen fit to spare me for*

---

*The Supreme Court did not rule on this issue before her execution. Previously the Court had established that persons who unalterably opposed capital punishment may not sit on juries that might be called to recommend the death sentence, but criteria had not been established for potential jurors with mixed feelings. In the Barfield case, one prospective juror said he did not know of any circumstance in which he might change his mind. This issue came to the Supreme Court at the same time as Wainwright *vs.* Witt, a capital-offense case in which a jury candidate was excluded after expressing mixed feelings. Prosecutors against Velma argued that her case was not the same because the person in her case said he would not change his mind.

now. Make these days meaningful. Use me so that these days won't be wasted.

I reread one of my special letters from Ruth Graham, dated February 2, 1984, one of the first she ever wrote to me:

> It is not easy, sitting on the outside, to express one's feelings adequately to one sitting on the inside.
>
> Let me just say, your letters, your attitude, your spirit of acceptance and humility, your relationship to our Lord, blesses one.
>
> And thank you, Velma, for including Bill and me in your early morning prayers. We need them....
>
> How reassuring to know that the past is under the blood of Christ and the future is in His hands. We all sit on death row, only for some it is more "definite" than others.
>
> The important thing you have already discovered is to know one has been forgiven by God because of Jesus's death on the cross in our place, and to live obediently with him.
>
> Whatever assails us here in the future...we'll meet in heaven, if not here.

I had to make plans for my funeral. An old friend came to the prison, and we talked about what I wanted done at my funeral. When he came in, I thought of the years he had been associated with us in our family, even as far back as when Thomas died.

"Well, Velma, we've been through some tough times together," he said.

I felt crushed when he said those words. He meant them kindly, but I could only think of the times I had been to his funeral home with the people I had killed. It wasn't easy for me to face him. I had known of his coming, of course, so that morning I had spent an extra-long time in prayer, asking God to give me the strength and courage for this ordeal.

I could have asked for someone else, but he had been with me through many dark times. He has that air of business about him when it has to be business. But when it's time for tenderness and compassion, he knows how to express it. He acted the same way that morning.

I hoped that my funeral would be a private affair. I was not trying to hide anything. After all, everybody knew what I'd done. I was thinking of the hurt for the kids and that it would be a lot easier for all my family if the news media didn't show up. But he, along with Jimmie and Chaplain Carter, helped me realize I couldn't prevent their coming.

I wanted to be alone for a while. I knew the people from the *Sixty Minutes* television show would be coming that afternoon, and I had less than two hours before their arrival.

Back in my cell I opened my Bible to Psalm 91, and as I read the first two verses, an inner peace came over me:

He who dwells in the secret place of
the Most High
Shall abide under the shadow of the
Almighty.
I will say of the LORD, "He is my
refuge and my fortress;
My God, in Him I will trust."

I poured out my heart to God. He knew the demands of the next few hours and that I had to do my best. I needed His added strength. Even though I didn't sleep, when I met with the people from *Sixty Minutes* I felt refreshed.

The court has set November 2 for my execution. I thought back in June when I went to Central Prison that I could deal with death one time and push it away. But I have to keep thinking about it because I can't escape. Everything around here keeps me facing this reality.

[*Editor's note:* The rest of this chapter refers to events beginning October 18, 1984.]

These last two weeks have been difficult—everything has changed. I'm constantly being taken out of my cell to see visitors, receiving mail in which people want to say good-bye and don't know how. I get no time for myself, and that makes it hard.

Every day I go through this disruption of schedule. I'm glad to see people and talk with them, but it also leaves me emotionally drained. Other prisoners have found excuses to come by my cell and talk a few minutes.

Last week a former guard came by to see me, and we spent over an hour together. "I had to come by and say good-bye, Miss Margie," he said. "You meant so much to me while I was working here. No matter how discouraged I got, you always had a smile for me, and you helped me through some of my difficult days."

Ronnie came on Saturday, October 20, and he brought Kim and her two children, Stacie and Wendy. I had a wonderful time with them, playing and laughing, and for long moments of time, forgetting the future.

The day before, Jimmie Little had bought a video camera and tape. He brought them in on Saturday morning. Jimmie spent that money just so that we could make video tapes of my last visit with the grandkids. After their time with me, Jimmie, wearing jeans and sports shirt, took the kids to the state fair and video-taped everything they did.

On Monday, October 22, exactly one week before my fifty-second birthday, the prison did a beautiful thing for me. I was allowed to have a birthday party with my special friends here at prison. We didn't know when I'd be taken to Central Prison, and the other ladies wanted to express their love for me before I left. They made me a birthday card almost two feet high and wrote messages all over it. They had so many messages from other prisoners that they had to keep adding extra pages.

They had two cakes on a table and all kinds of other party foods, and they filled the room with balloons. But the best part came when I saw the people who had played a special role in my life during my years on death row. Most of all, I saw my special little Beth along with all the others.

I kept fighting back tears, thinking that in one sense the last six years of life stood around me in that room. Those people had been with me during all or part of that time. I loved them all, and they made me feel very special.

Not only inmates came, but Chaplain Carter and Ms. Lancaster were there. One word kept going through my mind: family. This has been my special family and I've been so blessed.

On Tuesday, October 23, Jimmie brought the video tapes of Stacie and Wendy for me to see. That touched me deeply, but Jimmie covered up his generosity by saying, "I've been wanting to get one for a long time. You just gave me the excuse."

Anne Lotz received special permission to visit me Wednesday. I could hardly believe it, but we spent nearly three hours together. And I needed Anne that day. Maybe I needed a woman from outside who could sit and listen to another woman. She listened with compassion and seemed to know exactly what to say every time I paused.

We have run out of appeals. I told my attorneys that I want no more petitions merely for a stay of execution. If they can find cause for a new trial that can have some chance, that's different. But I don't want to continue putting off the date and waiting more days and months.

During these last weeks at women's prison, I have done a lot of reflecting on the past six years. Not only have I changed toward God and wanting to help other people, but I've changed in almost every way. I wish I could say that all my days in prison have been lived in peace. Almost every day I have struggled for an inner quietness. God has given it to me—after many battles.

These last days I feel emotionally drained from seeing people and having no time by myself. When I finally come back to my cell, too wearied to read or even to pray, I have found something helpful. Chaplain Carter loaned me a cassette player because Ruth Graham sent me tapes of some of the most beautiful Christian songs. I can lie on my bunk and listen to "O Love That Wilt Not Let Me Go" or "Jesus Shall Reign," and it gives me such calmness.

Some nights when I'm having trouble sleeping, I put the

player next to my ear and start one of the tapes. I drift off to sleep as I listen to a heavenly choir sing just for me.

One of the songs helped me as I found my mind dwelling on November 2. One of them says something about waking up and standing on the shores and discovering it's heaven. As I listened, I thought, *That's how it will be, Lord. I'll go to sleep and wake up and feel the touch of Your hand in mine.*

Perhaps as much as anything to make me face my final days, I had to decide on the form of death. The state of North Carolina offers the choice between cyanide gas and lethal injection.

I thought about it quite a bit. Even before the Central Prison warden, Nathan Rice, came to my cell with Jimmie to explain everything, Sam and Gales Roane had talked with me about it. Gales, a former nurse, helped me understand what I could expect.

Neither form causes pain. If I chose cyanide gas, I would have to sit up and face the witnesses as they strapped me in a chair. Then they would put a hood over my head, and I would breathe in the gas.

The lethal injection of a paralyzing drug, Pavulon, meant that they would first strap me onto a hospital gurney and then inject sodium pentothal to put me to sleep before giving me the fatal injection.

I tried to think of the children in making my decision because it won't make any difference to me. I decided that the lethal injection might be easier for them to observe. I urged Ronnie and Kim not to come to the execution. "I'd like your last memories of me to be the way it was at women's prison," I told them, "when I could sit and talk with you and play with the grandchildren."

Long ago I worked it out with Brother Hoyle, and we decided on the funeral. He will fly here before the execution, and he knows the Bible verses and the hymns I want sung. Sam Roane will sing one of my favorites, "His Eye Is on the Sparrow."

I have arranged to have any usable part of my body donated to a large university, but because of the paralyzing gas, this may not be possible. I decided that if God could use any part of me to help others, even in death, I wanted to do that.**

During these past few days, I have struggled for inner peace in the midst of confusion. I know the constant battle I have going on inside me—and I am winning. In the *Raleigh Times* of October 26, this was printed:

> Mrs. Barfield's emotional state is "probably better than everybody else's," her lawyer said. She is "not just sitting around thinking.... She is trying to a degree to answer most of the correspondence she has been getting, reading books and religious literature.... She has a very strong inner peace and she is dealing with this remarkably well," he said.

I am at peace because I am with Jesus Christ. I keep returning to the two verses that have sustained me from the beginning of my Christian life: "You will keep him in perfect peace, Whose mind is stayed on You, Because he trusts in You" (Isaiah 26:3) and "I will never leave you nor forsake you" (Hebrews 13:5).

No matter what happens now, I shall be with Jesus Christ forever.

**Because of the paralytic drug injected, Velma's kidneys could not be used. A spokesperson told her son, "We have enough good parts to benefit fifty people." Ronnie commented, "She would have liked that."

EPILOGUE

Two different groups gathered outside Raleigh's Central Prison on Thursday night, November 1, 1984.

In the early morning hours of November 2, Margie Velma Barfield's execution was carried out by lethal injection. She died at 2:15 A.M.

A spokesperson from the prison announced her death.

One group broke into jeers and cheers. Minutes later they disbanded.

The other—and larger—group of about two hundred people kept a vigil with lighted candles. Many of them had been in prayer for more than two hours before the execution.

"When I walked outside," the Reverend Hugh Hoyle said, "I saw them standing there, with their lighted candles, spelling out the word HOPE."

When relatives, friends, and supporters heard the announcement, they blew out the candles and someone started singing, "Amazing Grace." Soon all two hundred joined in, many sobbing between stanzas. Quietly they disbanded after the song.

Chaplain Carter told reporters, "Many of those at the Correctional Center for Women have told me that they never could have made it inside the prison if it hadn't been for 'Miss Margie,' Velma Barfield."

Chaplain Skip Pike, official chaplain at Central Prison, on the night of Velma's execution, said he was overwhelmed at times with the awesome responsibility of ministering to the thirty-nine men then on death row. He had been apprehensive about ministering to Velma. Not only was she a woman on death row, she was a woman facing imminent execution. When he walked into Velma's cell, however, Velma ministered to him as she read and expounded on the Scriptures the Lord had given to her for comfort and strength.

On Saturday, at her memorial service, Chaplain Carter said, "God reached out and touched and loved through Mrs. Velma Barfield. The Word became flesh in her. Lives were touched and lives were changed."

Chaplain Carter said that minutes before she was put to death, "Her face glowed. Her eyes were peaceful and content."

Following Velma's request made before her execution, Sam Roanes led the congregation in singing "Blessed assurance, Jesus is mine! Oh, what a foretaste of glory divine! Heir of salvation, purchase of God, born of His Spirit, washed in His blood. This is my story, this is my song, praising my Saviour all the day long." Sam's wife, Gales, played the organ with tears streaming down her cheeks. The Reverend Hoyle said, "She died with dignity and she died with purpose. Velma is a living demonstration of 'by the grace of God you shall be saved.' "

Ronnie Burke said, "She wanted to be known as a good Christian and nothing else."

The following poem was written by Ruth Bell Graham for Velma at the time of her execution. It did not arrive until the afternoon of November 2. The Reverend Hugh Hoyle read it for the benediction at Velma's funeral service.

As the eager parents wait
the homing of their child
from far lands desolate,
from living wild;
wounded and wounding along the way,
their sorrow for sin ignored,
from stain and strain of night and day
to home assured.

*   *   *

So the Heavenly Father waits
the homing of His child;
thrown wide those Heavenly Gates
in welcome glorious wild!
His, His the joy by right
—once crucified, reviled—
So—
Precious in God's sight
is the death of His child.

from Psalm 116:15

AFTERWORD

As I walked into the visitors' booth at Central Prison—North Carolina's maximum security institution for men—on June 30, 1984, having received permission to visit Velma Barfield before her scheduled execution on August 31, I was extremely apprehensive as to what I would find. From the various news reports, I knew something of her crimes; from her letters to my mother, I knew something of her professed faith in Christ; but as this was my first visit which I was making at my mother's request, I did not know Velma personally for herself.

What I discovered during that first forty-five minute visit was something I had not expected at all. When I inquired as to how she was, she sparkled as she replied that God's grace was sufficient. "Just as He has given me saving grace, just as He continues to daily give me living grace, I know He will give me dying grace" was her testimony. She then shared with me her terror at being transferred from the Women's Correctional Center to the death watch cell at Central Prison, having been given only thirty minutes to leave her cell—grabbing her nightgown, Bible, devotional book *(Joy and Strength)*, and a recent letter from my mother.

When she was placed in the small, windowless death watch cell across from the gas chamber, with a light bulb burning twenty-four hours a day and two guards constantly monitoring through a glass wall every move she made, her fear knew no bounds. She dropped to her knees, not even knowing how to pray, yet seeking the Lord's presence in her heart. As she remained on her knees, she said a deep peace crept over her, and the Lord seemed to remind her that several weeks earlier she had prayed for James Hutchins, living in that very cell, as he waited his execution—prayed that the Lord's presence would fill his cell and draw him to Himself. God seemed to say to Velma, "James Hutchins has left, Velma, but I haven't. I've been waiting to welcome you here."

As I left Central Prison after that initial visit, I knew I had been uniquely, richly blessed by a woman who not only was at peace with God, but who was radiantly alive in her love for Jesus Christ and absolutely triumphant over her circumstances. It was a discovery that caused me to be deeply drawn to her, resulting in many subsequent visits made possible by what turned out to be the final postponement of her execution date from August 31 to November 2, and her temporary return to the Women's Correctional Center.

Those visits became exceedingly precious to me because she always led me in worship of the Lord Jesus—not only by what she said, but by her attitude. She lived in Psalms 27 and 91, always seeing her circumstances through the knowledge of Christ's love for her, never judging His love for her by her circumstances. She constantly recognized His hand of love in her daily affairs and responded with even more love and gratitude because of it.

A few simple statements written in her Bible exemplify her attitude:

> My first execution date after my first round of appeals was set for October 17, 1980. October 9 God gave me another stay. Then another execution date was set for December 12, 1980. On December 3, 1980, God gave me another stay. December 31, 1980—I am fasting today—thanking and praising my God for all His blessings on me in 1980.

Velma Barfield lived humbly, gratefully, joyfully in her forgiveness by God and in His love for her. Following her execution, a reporter asked me what in the world did I have in common with a convicted murderer. I replied, "We were both in love with Jesus Christ."

On three separate occasions Velma told me, "If I had the choice of living free on the outside [of prison] without my Lord, or living on death row with Him, I would choose death row." As November 2 drew closer, her increasing longing to see the face of her beloved Lord took the sting of fear away.

As is true of all genuine disciples, she demonstrated her love for Christ by her obedience to His Word. The five following decisions she made were written in the flyleaf of her study Bible, dated October 30, 1981:

(1) Deal thoroughly with sin. Sin is being called all kind of fancy names nowadays but it's time we came to grips with ourselves and call sin what it really is—SIN. It's the ancient enemy of the soul. It has never changed. Tonight I'm making a new commitment to my Lord. I'm going to start tonight naming my sins before my Lord and *trust* Him for deliverance.

(2) Never own anything. I'm rededicating everything to my Lord—it's not mine to begin with—everything I own, everything I have here in this cell belongs to Him. He's loaned it to me to use. I'm saying here Lord—take my kids—they are not mine either—they belong to You and I'm leaving them in Your care—knowing that they will be well taken care of. I need not worry over them.

(3) Never defend myself. Father, tonight I'm turning over the defense of myself to You. I'm going to stop defending myself with Your help. I know You will defend me and no one will harm me. I am seeking to have a religious awakening within my spirit that will thrust me farther out into the deep things of God.

(4) Father, tonight, now, as I sit at your table—I know you expect to teach me table manners. So I'm making a new commitment to You to stop *passing anything on about anybody else that will hurt them*. A talebearer has no place in God's favor. I want you to be good to me, Father—so I must be good to Your children. So Yes You expect to teach me good table manners and You won't let me eat unless I obey the etiquette of the table. And the etiquette of the table is that I

don't tell stories about the brother who is sitting at the table with me.

(5) Never accept any glory. My God is jealous of His glory and He will not give it to another. Many want other people to know they are serving the Lord—this is dangerous ground—seeking a reputation among the saints. Father, I must determine that I will never take any glory, but see that You get it all.

Although I had not known of these decisions until after her execution when I was given access to her Bible, I saw them in evidence as she practiced them in her life.

Velma lived her life by God's Word. In going through her study Bible—one of several she used—I found that every page, with the exception of some in the book of Ezekiel, was marked. How many times she said to me, eyes sparkling, face radiant, "Anne, this Bible is where I get my strength. This is where my Lord speaks to me—I couldn't get up in the morning, much less go through the day, without His Word."

At one point, her testimony led me to share with her about the Bible class for women that I teach. As I described the disciplined study of God's Word, her face grew wistful. She said that she not only longed for such a class for herself, but for the other inmates at the Women's Correctional Center. She said that in fact she had been praying for a year and a half for a revival to take place within the prison population. We then bowed our heads, held hands, and prayed for just such a revival to take place, followed by the establishing of a Bible study class. As I left her that day, I told her possibly God would use her execution as a means to answer her prayer, and quoted to her John 12:24: "...except a grain of wheat fall into the ground and die, it remains alone; but if it die, it brings forth much fruit" (KJV).

I witnessed the execution of my dearly beloved sister in Christ on November 2, 1984, comforted by the knowledge that physical death is no interruption to a believer's relationship with Jesus Christ. It is merely a stepping over from a relationship based on faith, to one of sight. Velma Barfield, with peace and tranquility on her face, her lips moving in silent prayer, closed her eyes in death at 2:15 A.M. on November 2, while opening them to the face of her beloved Saviour and Lord for all eternity. Again, she led me in worship of the Lord Jesus Christ Who won the victory over death that we might know we have eternal life. Velma knew—and I knew—that she had eternal life, based on her faith in His Word.

The fruit has already begun to spring up. On December 5, one month following Velma's execution, my father, Billy Graham, led a service within the Women's Correctional Center, attended by every inmate and staff person the superintendent was able to have present. When he concluded his message of personal testimony weaved through John 3:16, two hundred and ten inmates and staff members responded to his invitation. After his message, he visited each inmate who had been unable to participate in the general meeting because of her security status. As he walked into the very cell block where Velma had been housed for the past three years, he found the inmates, who did not know he was coming, with their Bibles open, watching a television broadcast of his crusade. Velma's witness, even after her death, continues to permeate the very place she had lived.

As part of the follow-up to my father's visit that night, the Bible class known as Bible Study Fellowship has been invited by the superintendent and prison chaplain into the Women's Correctional Center. Practical arrangements are being made at this time to make it a reality within the next two months.

I have received countless notes and letters from those imprisoned—not physically, but spiritually—saying in effect that God has used Velma's radiant witness to help them understand, for the first time in their lives, His forgiveness of and love for them.

On December 15, 1984, I drove two hours to Velma's hometown of Lumberton, North Carolina, hand-carrying letters written by Velma to the families of her victims—expressing her sorrow and repentance, asking for their forgiveness, telling them of Christ's love. Having agreed by telephone to receive me, they refused when I arrived. They chose to remain blinded to the glory of God in Velma's life. That choice is also yours.

This testimony has been written that you might believe in the power of Jesus Christ to forgive any and all sin and to transform any and every life, as it has been demonstrated in the life of Velma Barfield. You may refuse to believe that she was forgiven or that her life was transformed; you may refuse to believe the power of Christ is available to forgive your sin and to transform your life today, but your refusal does not alter the truth—Velma Barfield was a woman on death row, set free by the power of Jesus Christ. And I am a grateful witness.

Anne Graham Lotz
February 1985

LIST OF

PRESCRIPTION DRUGS

Used by Velma Barfield, 1968–1978

All of the following are drugs which were prescribed for
Velma Barfield from 1968 to 1978. All of these drugs
have an effect on the brain and alter mental functioning.
These drugs range from major tranquilizers to mild antihista-
mines with sedative side effects. During her ten years of prescription drug abuse, she took multiple combinations of these
drugs, far greater than their prescribed dosages. Taken in recommended doses, most of these drugs stay active in the body
for days and some for weeks. Complete psychological withdrawal can take as long as one year. Taken in multiple doses
and combinations as Velma Barfield took them, the effect of
these drugs is magnified many times.

ANTIANXIETY AGENTS (TRANQUILIZERS)

Valium, *Traxene,* *Librium,* *Meprobam,* *Equagesic,* *Vis-
taril, Atarax, Benadryl*

Used for control of tension and anxiety. Should be used on
short term basic only. Selected side effects include depression,
acute hyperexcited states, confusion, rage, anxiety. The effect

of antianxiety agents is exaggerated when taken with barbiturates, narcotics, phenathiazines (Thorazine).

ANTIDEPRESSANTS

Elavil, Endep (highly sedating)
Sinequan (highly sedating), Tofranil (moderately sedating)

Eliminates feelings of hopelessness, helplessness, suicidal thoughts. Relieves sleep disorders, loss of appetite, fatigue. Selected side effects include confusional states, disturbed concentration, disorientation, delusions, hallucinations, excitement, anxiety, restlessness, insomnia, nightmares, incoordination.

ANTIPSYCHOTIC AGENTS (TRANQUILIZERS)

Thorazine

Used for (a) management of psychotic disorders; (b) control of excessive anxiety, tension, and agitation; and (c) control of symptoms associated with acute drug withdrawal. Contraindicated in the presence of large amounts of barbiturates or narcotics. May induce severe sedation and psychotic symptoms.

BARBITURATES

Seconal,* Butisol,* Phenobartital,* Fiorinal*

Highly sedating; used to induce sleep and reduce tension. Selected side effects include severe depression of the central nervous system, paradoxical excitement. Central nervous system depressive effect may be addictive with that of other central nervous system depressants.

NARCOTICS

Demerol,* Percodan* (relief of moderate to severe pain)
Tylenol with Codeine,* Darvon* (relief of mild to moderate pain)

Selected side effects include euphoria, dysphoria, agitation, disorientation, confusion, anxiety. Should be used with great caution in patients who are concurrently receiving other narcotics, tranquilizers, sedative-hypnotics (including barbiturates), and antidepressants. When combined with these may exhibit addictive central nervous system depression.

SLEEPING PILLS (NON-BARBITURATE HYPNOTICS)

Doriden,* Dalmane*

Used for relief of insomnia. Selected side effects include paradoxical excitation, apprehension, irritability, euphoria, depression, confusion, restlessness. Combined effects with other central nervous system depressants.

STIMULANTS (AMPHETAMINES)

Sanorex*
Other "diet" pills

Used for weight reduction. Selected side effects include nervousness, insomnia, overstimulation, dysphoria, restlessness. Contraindicated in people in agitated states or with a history of drug abuse.

---

*Drugs marked with an asterisk are addictive. All information on drug use and side effects is taken from the *Physicians' Desk Reference*, a compilation of the drug package inserts supplied by the drug companies themselves. The PDR® is published by the Medical Economics Company in Oradell, New Jersey.